By Land and By Sea:

Quakers Confront Slavery and its Aftermath in North Carolina

Hiram H. Hilty

Foreword by Lindley S. Butler

Illustrations by Mary Smith

Copyright © 1993 by Hiram H. Hilty

All rights reserved. No part of this book may be reproduced, stored in a retrieval system, or transmitted, in any form or by any means, electronic, mechanical, photocopying, recording, or otherwise, without prior written permission, except for brief quotations in connection with a literary review. For information address the North Carolina Yearly Meeting of Friends, 5506 Friendly Avenue, Greensboro, NC 27410.

First printed in 1984 as *Toward Freedom for all: North Carolina Quakers and Slavery*. Revised and expanded 1993.

Library of Congress Cataloging–in–Publication Data
Hilty, Hiram H.
    By land and by sea : Quakers confront slavery and its aftermath in North Carolina / Hiram H. Hilty ; foreword by Lindley S. Butler.
       p.   cm.
    Includes bibliographical references and index.
    ISBN 0-942727-22-3
    1. Slavery--North Carolina--History--18th century. 2. Slavery--North Carolina--History--19th century. 3. Quakers--North Carolina--History--18th century. 4. Quakers--North Carolina--History--19th century. 5. Slavery and the church--Society of Friends. 6. North Carolina--Race relations. 7. North Carolina--Church history.
I. North Carolina Friends Historical Society. II. Title.
E445.N8H54   1993
975.6'00496--dc20   93-34209

Cover engraving: Picture Collection, The Branch Libraries, New York Public Library.

Copyright Permission

Grateful acknowledgement is made to Friends United Press for permission to quote from and expand upon *Toward Freedom for All,* 1984.

Manufactured in the United States of America.
Composed by Friendly Desktop Publishing.
Printed by Thomson–Shore

```
975.6 H656b

Hilty, Hiram H.

By land and by sea
```

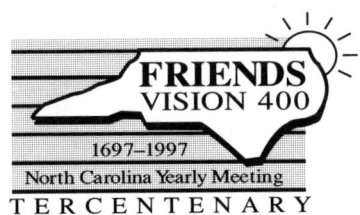

TERCENTENARY

A VISION 400 PUBLICATION

Starting in 1993 a series of events, exhibits, publications and projects will commemorate the 300th anniversary of the establishment of North Carolina Yearly Meeting, the annual gathering for members of the Society of Friends (Quakers).

Titled "Vision 400" to highlight the two North Carolina Yearly Meetings' first steps into their fourth century, the tercentenary celebration will culminate in a joint 300th yearly meeting session in the summer of 1997.

PUBLISHED BY:
NORTH CAROLINA FRIENDS HISTORICAL SOCIETY
P.O. BOX 8502, GREENSBORO, NC 27419
NORTH CAROLINA YEARLY MEETING OF FRIENDS
5506 FRIENDLY AVENUE, GREENSBORO, NC 27410

OTHER BOOKS BY THE AUTHOR

Friends in Cuba, 1977.

New Garden Friends Meeting: The Christian People Called Quakers, 1983.

Toward Freedom for All: North Carolina Quakers and Slavery, 1984.

Greensboro Friends Meeting, A New Meeting for a New Age, 1987.

DEDICATION

To our grandchildren: Debora Feagins Yousef, Colette Searls, Peter Searls and Elizabeth Chatfield.

Preface

It seems abundantly clear to us today that there is a contradiction between the beliefs of the Religious Society of Friends (Quakers) and the institution of slavery. For a very long time this was not clear to the rank and file of the Quaker community, for they quietly became a part of the system in the seventeenth and eighteenth centuries. From New England to Georgia, as Quakers prospered, many of them acquired slaves. By the middle of the eighteenth century, the more sensitive souls among them became troubled. In mid–life John Woolman became so concerned that he devoted the rest of his short life to the crusade against slavery. His influence was felt most strongly in Philadelphia, Maryland, and Virginia Yearly Meetings, but he also visited North Carolina in 1746 and 1757. Although it is true that New England declared slaveholding a disownable offense in 1715, and Philadelphia "testified against" slavery in 1696, the practice clearly continued. Otherwise, why would it have been necessary for Woolman to confront Quaker slaveholders up and down the British colonies throughout his ministry from 1743 to 1772? Even in the 1820s, the slavery question was a contributing factor in the Hicksite division, an important theological division among Friends at that time.

In the Carolinas, the slavery question became important somewhat later than in the northern colonies–states. In North Carolina, the focus of this study, freeing slaves was complicated by the unbending opposition of the local authorities and the state legislature. Although much influenced by the views of the wider Quaker community, North Carolina Quakers had to work out their own problems in unique ways, as we shall see. They did, however, receive much help from northern and "western" Friends.

As in the 1984 edition of *Toward Freedom For All: North Carolina Quakers and Slavery,* published by the Friends United Press, I acknowledge the encouragement and assistance of the late Dorothy Gilbert Thorne, J. Floyd Moore, E. Daryl Kent, the late Algie I. Newlin and Herbert Poole of Guilford College, and the late Professor Robert H. Woody of Duke University. For this edition, special thanks are due to Rausie Hobson, Joan Poole, Carole Treadway, Gertrude Beal and Nita Hilliard Smith for their careful reading of the manuscript and their helpful suggestions. Dot Kearns has given generously of her time to acquaint me with the High Point Normal and Industrial Institute. B. J. Weatherby has been the indispensable expert–friend in designing and preparing this book.

Hiram H. Hilty
Guilford College
August 2, 1993

Contents

Illustrations xi
Foreword xiii

Chapter

I. Thomas Newby Faces a Dilemma 1

II. The Nature of American Slavery 8

III. How It Started 19

IV. Caesar and God 26

V. Quaker Free Negroes 31

VI. Back to Africa. Haiti 34

VII. The Manumission Society. Bridges 41

VIII. Quakers in Court 44

IX. The Julius Pringle 57

X. Resettlement in Other States 67

XI. The Underground Railroad 72

XII. The Civil War 81

XIII. After the War 94

XIV. Unfinished Business 105

Endnotes 114

Bibliography 119

Index 123

About the author 135

Illustrations

	Page
Minute of Perquimans Monthly Meeting, April 6, 1774	2
Prince Henry the Navigator in Lisbon Harbor	9
Mother and child at slave auction	17
Many runaway slaves fled to the Dismal Swamp of North Carolina and established house camps	18
The Fox–Edmundson plaque at Hertford, North Carolina	20
The New Garden Meeting House of 1791	23
The Joseph Jordan Manumission Paper of 1784 (Photocopy of ms. original)	29
Portrait of Judge William Gaston	32
Quaker Free Negro refuses to go to Haiti	35
Quaker Free Negroes board ship for Liberia in Norfolk, VA	37
Quaker Free Negroes abandon barge frozen in canal	39
Portrait of William Swaim, opponent of slavery, editor of the *Greensboro Patriot*	42
Joe longs for slave bride he left behind in Kentucky	49
Philadelphia crowd demonstrates against black refugees from North Carolina	61
Jonas Mace waves farewell to Quaker Free Negroes en route to Liberia	63

YOUNG FRIENDS CARAVAN CONDUCTS SLAVES TO FREEDOM IN INDIANA	68
ROUTES TO LIBERTY OF QUAKER FREE NEGROES	70
PORTRAIT OF LEVI AND KATIE COFFIN	73
THE HOME AND INN OF RICHARD MENDENHALL IN JAMESTOWN, NORTH CAROLINA	78
LEVI COFFIN IS REMEMBERED IN GREENSBORO, NC	80
HARRIET LANE FOLLOWS FLAG OF TRUCE TO BALTIMORE	90
MAP SHOWING NORTHWEST TERRITORY AND FUTURE STATES	95
SOLOMON BLAIR'S SCHOOL FOR NEGROES IN HIGH POINT	99
JAMES'S PLANTATION SCHOOL, NORTH CAROLINA	100
TEACHING THE FREEDMEN	101
WILLIAM PENN AUDITORIUM, A NATIONAL HISTORIC PLACE	103
PLAQUE HONORING YARDLEY WARNER IN GREENSBORO	109

Foreword

This work, a revision of the author's *Toward Freedom for All* (1984) again brings before the public the little-known story of North Carolina Quakers' confrontation of slavery and racism. Among the southern states only North Carolina, with it long-settled Quaker community, had any consistent opposition to slavery throughout the antebellum period. From the days of the earliest settlement, Quakers, following their particular testimonies of pacifism and equality, had been an irritant to colonial authorities through public protest, tax resistance, and refusal to do military duty. Their commitment to religious equality, which was bolstered by the secular natural rights political philosophy, was a central witness of their faith. Although gender equality was practiced by Quakers from their earliest days in the seventeenth century, it took nearly a hundred years for them to come to the realization that slavery also was morally wrong and that their witness for equality must cross racial lines.

The author begins his narrative with the manumission in 1777 of a group of Perquimans County slaves by Thomas Newby and others. Manumission, the individual freeing of a slave, became common among Quakers despite the local and state officials' practice of deporting the freed persons or attempting to reenslave them. To nullify the effect of deportation, the Yearly Meeting with legal advice from Judge William Gaston developed the unique response of protecting the ostensibly freed persons by assuming ownership of them while allowing them to live as freedmen.

Hilty deftly weaves an interesting story of Quaker involvement in manumission societies, in colonization movements of freedmen to Haiti and Liberia, in litigation in state and local courts on behalf of freedmen, and in the Underground Railroad to aid escapees. In an age when itinerant abolitionists were arrested and often deported, how did Quakers over several generations manage to confront openly the most sensitive sociopolitical issue of the times and yet be tolerated by the broader community? Quaker status in North Carolina as a dissenting minority had been won by a century and a half of residence in a state that from its inception attracted and tolerated political and religious dissenters. Initially slaveholders like their neighbors, Quakers had over a century evolved their abolitionist view, and their protest, while persistent, was essentially local and moderate. The state made allowances for the peculiar witnesses of Quakers, yet over the years as a dissenting minority they paid a price which ultimately led to the majority of the state's Quakers migrating to the region north of the Ohio River, especially to Indiana and Ohio.

After the Civil War the Quaker remnant suffered with the entire state the poverty and violence of the Reconstruction era. With the support of the Baltimore Association, relief was provided for those who remained and resources were made available to rebuild meetings and schools. The most notable Quaker educational achievement for blacks was the normal and industrial school in High Point that became the William Penn High School. According to Mary Mendenhall Hobbs, the Quakers were exhausted by the loneliness and isolation of their pre–war witness against slavery. As a result, North Carolina Friends, now more concerned with institutional survival, accepted the "separate but equal" condition of segregation. Trust between blacks and Quakers remained, but the thrust of the civil rights leadership in the mid–twentieth century would come from the blacks themselves with Quakers taking a secondary and sometimes a reluctant place in the social changes of the modern era.

To be a dissenter is never an easy choice, but by remaining true to their spirituality Quakers have often been the conscience of our society. The story that Hiram Hilty has told so well is the other side of the mainstream of Southern history. It deserves to be better known by Friends and by the general public, and this revision makes this story of moral courage and dissent more accessible to all.

Lindley S. Butler
Wentworth, NC
June 17, 1993

I

Thomas Newby Faces a Dilemma

The Declaration of Independence really meant: All white males are created equal.

We will begin our story with Thomas Newby, a Quaker planter and business man living on the coastal plain of northeastern North Carolina in 1774. His home was near the Chowan River, not far from Hertford, the place where William Edmundson and George Fox first brought the Quaker message a hundred years before. We begin with Thomas Newby because he is the first North Carolina Quaker planter of record to declare publicly before his friends gathered in their monthly meeting for business that he planned to free his slaves. On April 6, 1774, it was written in the minutes of Perquimans Monthly Meeting that Thomas Newby declared that he was "uneasy on account of slave-keeping and requested the advice and assistance of friends" in liberating his slaves in a responsible manner.

Thomas's concern weighed heavily on the assembled Friends. Some of them also owned slaves, and it was becoming clearer every day that this was against all the things that Friends professed to believe. Yet, it was also clear that freedom presented serious problems for the slaves in the short term. How could they earn a living for themselves after having been dependent on their "owners" all their lives? What was to prevent their being forced back into slavery by unscrupulous slave traders? There was no clear answer to such questions, so Perquimans Friends decided the matter was too *those parts was a[t] this meeting and produced a certificate from the monthly meeting held at Hampton in the province of New hampshire in New England dated the 17th of 6th month 1773. Likewise her companion Elizth Southwick produced a certificate from the monthly Meeting held at Smithfield in New England dated 26th of ye 8th mo 1773. Also Benjamin Hough an assistant companion of our abovesaid friends produced a certificate from the monthly meeting held in Wilmington dated the 10th of 11th month 1773. all which were to Satisfaction, and friends appoints Wm Albertson and Benjamin Albertson to prepare certificates for the abovesaid friends in order to be signed at the Next Quarterly Meeting. — Also Miriam Elliott being Lately deceas'd and Left two children which coming under the notice of this meeting, friends think proper to appoint Jonathan Pearson and Wm Newby to take care that they are bound out to persons Suitable. ——*

Also our friend Thomas Newby being uneasy on account of Slave keeping Requested the advice & Assistance of friends in the weighty and Important affair of giving them their Liberty and this meeting thinks proper that the case be laid before the standing committy. ——

Nothing further offering needfull to record the meeting concluded and adjourns to the Next in course.

A portion of the minutes which record that Thomas Newby brought the issue of slave–keeping to the Perquimans Monthly Meeting. Friends Historical Collection, Guilford College.

"weighty" for them and referred it to the yearly meeting for advice.

For its part, the North Carolina Yearly Meeting had been struggling with this problem for some years. Gradually, they had reached the point where they admonished all Friends to manumit their slaves. They supported Thomas Newby's proposal. Other hearts had been touched, and three years later, in 1777, Thomas Newby decided that the time had come to act: He freed his slaves. Ten other Friends joined him in this courageous act, which reverberated across the coastal plain and provoked the attention of the courthouse, the statehouse, and was even debated in Congress. Between them, the eleven Quaker planters eventually freed 134 slaves. They had eased their consciences, and freedom had dawned for 134 children of God with dark skins.

The Friends joining Thomas Newby in this historic act were "Caleb White, Joseph Henley, Sach. Nixon, Benj. Albertson, Wm. Albertson, Chalkley Albertson, George Walton and Thomas White." Who were these courageous souls who braved the disapproval of the government officials, and apparently a preponderance of the local establishment? The indication is that they were solid, sober citizens, who by dint of hard work and right living had accumulated a generous portion of this world's goods. Indeed, some of them lived so comfortably, that John Woolman and other Quaker visitors were disturbed that they lived so well on the labor of slaves.

Thomas Newby, especially, is still remembered in the old Quaker community of Belvidere, near Hertford. He was an overseer and elder in his Friends meeting and owned an estate said to have reached 1,000 acres. Furthermore, he owned a store at Newby's Bridge and had a wharf where his own ocean–going vessels were said to have docked.[1] Some credit him with having built the historic Belvidere House. A public stand against slavery, including emancipation of his own slaves, was sure to attract a lot of attention in the community.

Another name that stands out among those who freed their slaves is Thomas Nicholson. Nicholson was a recorded minister and missionary who wrote abolitionist tracts. He reports a visit to Governor Gabriel Johnston. His ministry even carried him to England in 1749–1751, where he engaged in missionary activity. While there he called on Lord Granville, whose lands in the Piedmont were settled by Quaker immigrants from Pennsylvania and Nantucket. These were the Cane Creek and New Garden settlements. Granville received Nicholson graciously and expressed his pleasure at having so many Friends settling on his estates.[2]

The other persons releasing their slaves with Thomas Newby continued in the effort to gain freedom for all slaves. Their names recur frequently in the long struggle that was to follow.

At the time of the manumissions in Perquimans County, great events were occurring in the other American colonies. Three years earlier, the Declaration of Independence had been approved by the Continental Congress, in which it had been declared that "all men are created equal." Yet, in fact, the meaning was that all white males were created equal.

African–American persons still wore the chains of bondage and would continue to do so for eighty–five more years. Thomas Jefferson, the author of the Declaration of Independence, was one of those who saw the hypocrisy in this, but the excitement of the rebellion against England prevented rational action. Independence came first, and freedom for the slaves would have to wait. If slaves got too excited about freedom, they might join the British enemy against the colonists.

Indeed, slaveholders always feared slave rebellion, and it was this fear that bred the harsh laws to keep the slaves in check. Even the kindly Moravians at Salem, who accepted an occasional black member into their fellowship, kept a store of gunpowder on hand to use in case of a slave rebellion. And so it was that the act of freeing the slaves in Perquimans County became a source of great consternation and fear for many white persons in that place. The sheriff rounded up the freed slaves and put them up for sale on the courthouse steps. In view of this, the Quakers began to buy back their freed slaves to keep them out of abusive hands and perpetual bondage. Seeing this, the court countered by offering a reward to persons who brought in slaves "illegally" freed by Quakers. The North Carolina Yearly Meeting of Friends responded by hiring lawyers to defend the freedmen.

The cat and mouse game of Quakers freeing their slaves, only to have them picked up by the sheriff, went on for years. In the North Carolina State Archives in Raleigh is the following notice in the materials from Perquimans County:

> Sheriff's notice of sale of above who were taken up under the Act of Assembly, for passing as free negroes, supposed to have been manumitted by their former owners, John Anderson, Joshua Moore and Elihue Albertson. The former owners are summoned to court, April 5, 1785, agreeable to the Act of Assembly in that case provided.
> — Charles Moore.
>
> The endorsement says "to be sold tomorrow at 12 o'clock."

As will appear from the above, the Perquimans County Court had prevailed upon the state legislature to pass a law specifically making it a crime to free a slave without approval of the county court. Further, the law stated that the Quaker manumissions of 1777 were illegal.

How could one get court approval for freeing a slave? By proving that a slave had performed "meritorious service." This might be something like saving a white person from drowning, or from being gored by a bull, or from being killed by a wild beast. In other cases, it might be simply long and faithful care of an aged white person, and, indeed, this accounted for most manumissions. It was up to the court to decide. Yet, before the revolutionary troubles, even infants were manumitted sometimes for "meritorious service," whatever that might have meant.

Court records indicate that there were some persons in Perquimans and Pasquotank counties who made it a business to round up freed slaves. Thomas Creecy and William Arrington seem to have been among those who probably thought it a patriotic duty, as well as a good source of income, to haul in the manumitted slaves as fast as they were released by the Quakers.

How could it be, some might ask, that any Quakers at all still held slaves as late as 1777? The first public protest against slavery came to the Philadelphia Yearly Meeting of Friends from a congregation of Quakers and Mennonites in Germantown, Pennsylvania, in 1688, and eight years later the yearly meeting itself "testified" against slavery, thus making it a violation of discipline for members to own slaves.

In 1715, New England Yearly Meeting declared that Quakers would be disowned if they kept slaves. Epistles and visitors brought this news to North Carolina. Antislavery advocates such as John Woolman of New Jersey visited North Carolina and brought strong antislavery messages. Yet, these messages were only occasional, and journals of the time emphasize the remoteness of the Quaker settlements of North Carolina and the great difficulty of traveling there. North Carolina remained largely isolated from the centers of American Quakerism in Philadelphia and New England. In their yearly meetings, North Carolina Friends held the epistles from London Yearly Meeting in especially high regard and often had them printed and distributed in the monthly meetings. In these epistles, London Friends admonished North Carolina Friends to free their slaves, but London was far away and some questioned whether English Friends really understood the American situation.

The situation was that North Carolina was much more deeply enmeshed in the use of slave labor than the North. The Southern economy, whether dominated by the cultivation of tobacco or cotton, had been tied to slave labor from the beginning. It was specifically authorized by the Fundamental Constitutions of Carolina issued in 1669. Handed down from father to son for generations, slavery must have seemed as natural as breathing.

The thing that apparently brought eastern Friends to a conviction of the sin of slavery was the concern of Friends from Pennsylvania who settled in piedmont North Carolina in the mid–1700s. It was the insistence of these Friends that caused them to examine their consciences in the light of the gospel they professed. Of course the urgings of visiting Friends from William Edmundson and George Fox to John Woolman were also a factor. In any case, the decision of North Carolina Friends to rid themselves of the taint of slavery and to labor for the end of that institution was firm and would remain so until the Proclamation of Emancipation finally settled the matter.

II

THE NATURE OF AMERICAN SLAVERY

American slavery was essentially a monster born out of time. The Christian societies of Europe had largely turned away from slavery at the time it began to flourish in the American colonies. It was regarded as a vestige of an unenlightened era, although commercial interests deemed it appropriate for colonies in remote places.

Shakespeare gives us a glimpse of race attitudes in sixteenth century Venice, in his play *Othello*. Othello, a black man, is married to a high-born Venetian woman and appears as a military genius in command of Venetian troops. Tragedy destroys both Othello and Desdemona, but the honorable Othello is no slave.

As we step farther back in time, however, we find slavery present everywhere. The Bible contains counsel for the treatment of slaves, and the Apostle Paul advised Onesimus to return to his master. Yet, it is precisely in Paul's writings that we find an eloquent statement of the universality of the Christian gospel that makes slavery impossible for the Christian, assuming that practice follows theory. To the Galatians he wrote: "There is no longer Jew nor Greek, there is no longer slave nor free, there is no longer male and female: for ye are all one in Christ Jesus."[3]

In secular history, we find slavery prominent in both Greece and Rome. Native Americans enslaved prisoners of war, and indeed most slavery in all ages had its origin in warfare. One of John Woolman's strong arguments against slavery was that it was based on war, by which captives were reduced to slavery.

The roots of American slavery are in Portugal. As the Portuguese ventured ever farther down the west coast of Africa during the 1400s in defiance of warnings that the water was boiling at the equator and that human life was impossible in such a place, they eventually made contact with the black population of equatorial Africa. Upon their return to Portugal, they brought African captives with them, whom they sold as slaves in Portugal and other parts of Europe.

Statue of Prince Henry the Navigator in Lisbon Harbor. Portugal opened the gates of black Africa to Europe and America.

The Portuguese were the leading navigators of the world in the 1400s. Christopher Columbus went first to King John II of Portugal to get sponsorship for his great adventure across the Ocean Sea. The wise counselors of the king knew that the distance around the globe was much greater than Columbus supposed and rejected the idea. Nevertheless, Isabella of Spain allowed herself to be persuaded by the romantic Genoan and agreed to finance the venture. Her ignorance brought fame and fortune to Spain.

When Columbus arrived in the New World, he enticed some of the natives aboard ship and took them back to Spain with him. There, in a famous ceremony at Barcelona, he reported on his historic voyage and offered his "Indian" hostages as slaves to the queen. The pious Catholic Queen, however, rejected the offer and instructed Columbus to return them to the New World and set them free. Nevertheless, the Spanish colonists who settled the newly discovered islands ignored the Queen's advice and reduced the native population to a system of forced labor that became an especially oppressive form of slavery. These gentle people, accustomed to an easygoing form of life in the benign tropics, began to run away to the forests, while others chose to jump into the ocean and drown rather than to submit to slavery. In the end, almost the entire native population of the islands died.

In the midst of those terrible times, a Catholic priest, by the name of Bartolome de las Casas, spoke out against the planters and in defense of the Indians. His daring brought fierce opposition from the Spanish colonists, but he persisted and finally got the attention of the Spanish crown, and laws were decreed protecting the Indians. Las Casas carried his crusade to the North American continent and eventually became the bishop of the Mexican province of Chiapas. But it was too late for the Caribbean natives. For his unflagging devotion to the welfare of the natives, Las Casas was honored by the Spanish Crown with the title of Protector of the

Indians and is so revered throughout Latin America today.

Ironically, this good man set in motion events leading to African slavery in America. Observing the plight of the natives, he suggested importing African laborers since they were larger and stronger and more suited to heavy work. The Caribbean planters were pleased with this arrangement. In his zeal to protect the natives, Las Casas thus became an instrument in fixing African slavery on the American continent. Spain developed a lucrative business importing slaves into the western hemisphere and continued its monopoly until forced to share it with the British. The role of Las Casas in introducing African slavery to America has not been lost to African–American students of these events, and it is understandable that they are often hostile to the Spanish priest.

The first African slaves went to the Caribbean islands, but as the European population increased in North America many were sent there from the islands. Up until the very end of the slave trade, many slaves on American plantations had spent a year or two in Cuba for "seasoning," to get used to the climate and customs of slavery in the western hemisphere.

The majority of African slaves were prisoners of war; indeed, the slave trade set off a wave of wars in Africa, which were often instigated for the very purpose of capturing slaves. Slave ships were virtual torture chambers, with rows of shelves where captives remained prone in quarters too tight to even sit up. Some managed to jump overboard to their death rather than face a lifetime of slavery in a strange land. Sometimes slaves mutinied, killed the captain and crew, and captured the ship.

Some slaves, like the ancestors of author Alex Haley, were kidnapped in Africa and sent to America, suffering a fate similar to that of prisoners of war. By the 1800s in North America, there were millions of slaves who were American born and knew no other life than that of the slave.

Stories about life on the plantations abound, but there are also accounts from memories of former slaves, and from contemporary records scattered about in printed sources. It varied greatly from one plantation to another. Alex Haley brought the realities of slave life to the attention of twentieth century Americans in a forceful way in his book *Roots* and the film based on it. There were contemporary novels like Harriet Beecher Stowe's *Uncle Tom's Cabin*, published in 1852, and first-hand descriptions like Helper's *The Impending Crisis in the South*, published in 1857.

Our twentieth century impression of slavery oscillates from that of a benign institution, until recently the view propagated in southern schools, to the image of perpetual terror common in northern schools. Both contained more than a little truth. Among the "good" plantations of which we have record was that of Dr. James Green Carson of Mississippi. Dr. Carson was a religious man who became convinced of the sinfulness of slavery and made plans to free his slaves, but Mississippi law, as that of North Carolina at the time, prohibited him from doing so. Failing in that effort, he set about improving the condition of his slaves. He hired a doctor to look after their health, paid white missionaries to come and preach to them on Sundays, used labor-saving machinery to make work less burdensome for them, and never used the whip.[4]

Clearly, Dr. Carson's plantation was exceptional, but we are told that it was not unusual for owners to provide medical care; a sick slave was of no use to his master. Food, clothing, and shelter varied greatly according to the affluence of the planter and his character. Frederick L. Olmsted, the respected New York journalist, architect, and social planner, wrote from Richmond, Virginia, that the slaves he saw there were "probably better fed than the proletarian class of any other part of the world." Housing and clothing, he reported, were extremely modest, but not totally inadequate.[5]

In contrast, Josiah Hinson spoke of the great privations on the Maryland plantations where he lived as a boy. "Two regular meals a day (three in harvest); lodged in log huts and on bare ground; wind, snow, rain blew through the cracks and turned the floors to mud in winter."[6] Harriett Tubman, the famous antislavery activist, grew up a slave in Maryland and confirmed Hinson's description. Sometimes slaves lived in long sheds, as many as thirty living together. In other cases they had family-style cabins, so well known to us from stories and pictures of slave days. Sometimes the cabins housed three or four persons, but at other times there might be as many as ten or twelve crowded into them.[7]

There were lighter moments interrupting the heavy daily work, at least on some plantations. At Christmas and certain other holidays the slaves were allowed to have music, dancing, and games, although on the Quaker plantations certain constraints were imposed to avoid immoral practices. Frederick Douglass, the famous ex-slave who spoke extensively, especially in New England, of his plantation experiences, reported that as a boy he was free to do whatever he pleased and had a very happy childhood. "It was a long time," he said, "before I knew myself to be a slave."[8]

"Aunt" Betty Cofer recalled her life as a slave with a Jones family at Bethania, North Carolina, in an interview with the Federal Writers' Project in 1939. She was then in her seventies, which would have made her a mere child at the end of the Civil War. Nevertheless, her memories, nurtured by those of her family, were fond ones. At the time of the interviews she continued her friendship with members of the Jones family whom she had known all her life. She had married a man who worked in the R.J. Reynolds Tobacco Factory in Winston-Salem and had enjoyed a life of relative security and fulfillment.

The black and white communities interacted with one another in many ways. Between them they created the Southern dialect of the English language. The influence of the black "mammy" on white children was profound. Often the children spent more time with these surrogate mothers than with their birth mothers. The "mammies" often breast-fed the white babies and continued taking care of them for years. The bonding between the two became intense, color being no barrier to warm, human affection. In later years, these white children–become–adults often protected their foster mothers from abusive parents or cruel overseers.[9]

Although it often seemed to the Quakers that they were alone in perceiving the humanity of the slaves, there were, in fact many others, often lonely and courageous persons. In 1850, for example, the Reverend J. H. Thornwell preached a courageous sermon at the dedication of a church in South Carolina. He concluded by saying: "but the instinctive impulse of our nature, combined with the plainest declarations of the Word of God, lead us to recognize in his [i.e., the Negro's] form and lineaments — his religious and intellectual nature — the same humanity in which we glory as the image of God. We are not ashamed to call him our brother."[10]

Among the organized groups in North Carolina who opposed slavery was a small religious community on the northern fringes of the piedmont Quaker community known as the Nicholites. They flourished in the early 1800s, eventually being absorbed in part by the Quakers. The Nicholites used the following query (a reminder of the Quaker view) on slavery:

> Are friends careful to bear a steady testimony against slavery and oppression in all its different branches, endeavoring in everything to do to others as we in like case would have others do to us?[11]

There were certainly ample humanitarian reasons, as well as religious ones, to oppose slavery. John Woolman remarked in his letter to the New Garden and Cane Creek meetings in 1757 that:

> Where slaves are purchased to do our labour, numerous difficulties attend it. To rational creatures bondage is uneasy and frequently occasions sourness and discontent in them, which affects the family and such who claim mastery over them, and thus people and their children are many times encompassed with vexations which arise from applying wrong methods to get a living.[12]

Woolman's assertion that slavery made "rational creatures... uneasy" is obvious enough. It is true also of animals such as horses who must be "broken" to the saddle or harness before they will submit to them. That is, the trainer must "break" the will of the animal to be free. In the same way, at least some slaves had to be "broken" in order to make slaves out of them. Frederick Douglass described his own experience: "Six months under a Negro breaker succeeded in breaking me. I was broken in body, spirit and soul." William Wells told of seeing a proud black man turned into "a degraded spirit — crushed man by three months of daily floggings and unremitting labor."[13]

Despite the instances of humane treatment that we have cited, there was obvious and blatant abuse on many plantations. One must also consider that pain is psychological as well as physical. Lunsford Lane, who was born a slave, reported that he had an early childhood similar to that of Frederick Douglass — carefree and playing with his master's white children without discrimination. At about ten years of age, however, he had to work. At that point everything changed. His old playmates ordered him around and he came to realize that he was, indeed, a slave. "Deep was the feeling," he said, "and it preyed upon my heart like a never dying worm."[14]

Certain types of behavior and certain moods of overseers brought floggings for many slaves. Probably most of these punishments were accepted without protest, but there were instances where slaves fought their masters. Sometimes they served notice that no white man would ever flog them, and they held their ground.[15]

Slaves complained often and bitterly about the separation of families, and this was an evil most commonly condemned by Quakers and abolitionists. Even when they were not separated by sale, husbands and wives often did not live together, because it was more than a man could bear to see his wife raped or beaten and not be able to defend her. As a consequence, men generally avoided marrying women on their own plantations but established bonds elsewhere, contenting themselves with occasional visits.[16]

Mary A. Hicks reports the story of a slave sale in Raleigh, North Carolina, as told to her in 1937 by a son of a witness. A slave woman was on the auction block, and she clutched a two–or three–year–old child to her breast. The successful bidder declared that he had no interest in the child and insisted that it be sold separately. The child was then snatched from the mother, and "the woman screamed and the other Negroes sobbed in sympathy." The happy ending was that a young white man, named William Holden, stepped forward, bought the child and "gave it to the mother as a free child." This young man was to become the first governor of North Carolina after the Civil War.[17] Levi Coffin recounts a similar story, adding that the mother sold at a high price, in part because the auctioneer described her as highly trustworthy because she was "a church member and a Christian."[18]

Sometimes runaway slaves established closed, small communities which they defended vigorously. The writer recalls visiting such a "Maroon" community, as it was called, in Jamaica. In that case, a tiny territory never surrendered to the invading British in 1655, and maintains its technical independence from the Jamaican government to this day.

Historian Herbert Aptheker quotes the claims of a group of planters in North Carolina in 1830. They declared that their "slaves are become almost uncontrollable. They go and come when and where they please, and if an attempt is made to stop them they immediately fly to the woods and there continue for months and years committing depredations on our Cattle, hogs and Sheep...patrols are of no use on account of the danger they subject themselves to...."[19]

Runaway slaves were sometimes welcomed by Native Americans. The Seminoles in Georgia and Florida intermarried with them and fought enthusiastically against the United States in the Seminole Wars (1835–1842).

William Holden returns a child to its mother at a slave auction.

In sum, life on the plantations, when not openly cruel, was perceived as bearable in an imperfect world by some slaves, but an unbearable tyranny by others. As time went on, and the abolition movement gained strength in the North, the dream of freedom soared on the plantations. When it finally came at the end of the war, it was greeted with jubilation by the slaves, belying the notion that they were blissfully happy with the "peculiar institution" that had just come to an end.

Many runaway slaves fled to the Dismal Swamp of North Carolina and established house camps such as the one above.

III

HOW IT STARTED

Quakers were among the first white settlers of North Carolina. When William Edmundson came from Ireland to North Carolina in 1672, he found a lonely Quaker, named Henry Phillips, and his wife, who claimed they had not seen a fellow Quaker in seven years. The Phillips family had come from Massachusetts and were overjoyed to receive a visitor, especially since he shared their Quaker faith.

Later in 1672, Edmundson returned to North Carolina with George Fox, who is deemed the founder of Quakerism. They held meetings among the inhabitants of coastal North Carolina, neighbors of Henry Phillips. A historic marker indicates the place at Hertford where this, the first recorded Christian service in North Carolina, was held by the Quaker missionaries.

As Edmundson viewed the scene in North Carolina, he was disturbed by the exploitation of Native Americans and African-Americans. In 1676, he wrote a letter to Friends in America in which he said: "And many among you count it unlawful to make slaves of the Indians: and if so, then why the Negroes?" Historian Thomas Drake says that this gives Edmundson first place among antislavery apostles.[20]

Fox's concern about human exploitation at the time of his visit to North Carolina was for Native Americans. However, on his journey to the North American colonies, he had visited the West Indian island of Barbados, and there he had been accused by the governor of stirring up the slaves against their masters. While he denied this charge, he did counsel slaveholders to use tenderness in the treatment of their charges.

Edmundson's reference to Quaker concern for the Indian is attested, among other places, in the journal of Thomas Story. In one case, Friends Roger Hill and Thomas Story visited the house of James Johns at Burleigh in eastern North Carolina in 1699. Story "was exercised over the welfare of some Indian servants," and "unfolded to them spiritual things."[21]

Again Story visited the Chickahominy tribe where he found the "Sagamor or chief" a "grave, serious and wary old man." Nevertheless, Story gained his confidence, and through him was able to speak to an assembly of villagers about "the things of God." As they left they shook hands all around and they "seemed well pleased with our visit."[22]

It was in this world of Native American, white, and black that the Phillips family had settled, and the Quaker missionaries who

This Fox–Edmundson plaque is located in Hertford, Perquimans County, NC, a few yards from the bridge crossing the Perquimans River.

visited them created there the first organized religious group in the colony. When the Quaker manumissions were made in 1777, there had been Quakers in the North Carolina section of the coastal slave empire for more than a hundred years. There, they lived sober, industrious lives and prospered for four generations before the War of Independence. It transpired that in 1695, the newly appointed British governor of the Carolinas was a Quaker named John Archdale. He made no secret of his religious convictions and was in close touch with the fledgling Quaker community. He was committed to friendly relations with Native Americans, and his tenure was marked by a period of peace and understanding. Under Archdale, Quakers were excused from taking the oath and from serving in the military. The colonial council itself was dominated by Quakers, and it is said that some even sought membership with them to gain political advantage.

When Governor Archdale returned to England, he found himself elected to Parliament. However, when that body insisted that he take the oath of office, refusing to make an exception because of his faith, he declined to be seated in that august body. (Quakers refused to swear any kind of oath on principle.) Nevertheless, the memory of Archdale's benign governorship in the Carolinas remains. A town in Randolph County is named for him, and at Guilford College a building bears his name.[23]

The evidence is that the North Carolina Quaker community did not consist of religious refugees, with the possible exception of the Phillips family. The group was rather the product of the preaching of William Edmundson, George Fox, and other Quaker missionaries who followed them. Early visitors uniformly described the early settlers as simple farmer folk of less than elegant personal habits. In time, they were joined by Quakers from Virginia and other American colonies, with occasional ones from England and Ireland.

Situated as they were in the midst of the slave empire on a flat coastal plain well suited to plantation culture, they adopted the institution of slavery as a matter of course, until questions began to be asked within the larger Quaker family.

Of special importance in this process were the Quaker settlements at Cane Creek and New Garden, over 200 miles to the west in the present Alamance and Guilford counties. Most of these Friends had come from Pennsylvania and Virginia, and some from Nantucket Island, and were more closely in touch with the growing disapproval of slavery within the larger Quaker community. They brought with them the concerns of their mother yearly meetings. It seemed to them that North Carolina Friends took too lightly the advice of Quaker leaders about proper treatment of slaves, the education of slave children, and the provision of spiritual care of the blacks. Indeed, most of them thought it was wrong to own slaves at all, as their home yearly meetings had declared.

It should be remarked that compliance was imperfect in the North as well. John Woolman became an antislavery activist when he was asked to write a bill of sale for a black woman slave in New Jersey. Yet, the recent settlers in North Carolina were pained by a laxness among Friends in their attitudes toward slavery as it was practiced all around them.

At the New Garden Meeting in Guilford County the slavery matter weighed heavily on the conscience of Friends. The first meeting, under the authorization of Cane Creek Meeting, was held at the home of Thomas Beals in 1752. It turns out that Beals was much concerned about slavery. Stephen B. Weeks, in *Southern Quakers and Slavery,* tells us that at New Garden Beals "preached the crusade against slavery and proclaimed the West as a promised land." He took his own advice, for he later went west and settled at (old) Chillicothe, Ohio, where he is remembered as a pioneer missionary to the Indians.[24]

How It Started

An incident at the New Garden Meeting in 1767 seems to have stirred the piedmont settlements to action. The monthly meeting received a request for membership from one Obadiah Harris, a Friend who was transferring his membership from Cedar Creek Meeting in Virginia to New Garden. He had been living in the neighborhood long enough for New Garden Friends to know his living habits, and his reputation was not good. The first charge was that he was "of late being overtaken with strong drink."

Secondly, there was word that Obadiah was guilty of "selling a poor Negro slave, and parting him distant from his espoused Wife, and near connections sorely against his will, for which this meeting appointed John Hiatt and Richard Williams, to visit, and labor with him in love, and endeavor to inform his mind, the exceeding pernicious evils they are of...."[25]

The Friends appointed to labor with Obadiah Harris were successful in their mission and Friend Obadiah made amends to the slave he had wronged. All this probably came as something of a

New Garden Meetinghouse of 1791 Drawing by John Collins. Friends Historical Collection, Guilford College.

surprise to Obadiah, for Virginia was even more deeply enmeshed in the slave tradition than coastal North Carolina.

Another case came up in New Garden the same year. Jesse Henley brought a certificate of membership from the Pasquotank Monthly Meeting in Eastern Quarterly Meeting, where slavery had been in use for so long. However, the Pennsylvanians at New Garden objected to his membership request because he was accused of "having been concerned in the unchristian Trade of slave buying." Again a committee was appointed, and in due course Jesse Henley brought a paper to the monthly meeting condemning his conduct.[26]

All this so heightened Friends' sensibilities to the slave question that New Garden Friends went to the Western Quarterly Meeting and urged that the yearly meeting require Friends to refrain altogether from buying and selling slaves. When this request came to the North Carolina Yearly Meeting in 1770, it was too strong for the Friends there assembled. Instead, the meeting adopted a weak statement condemning the importation of slaves, restricting purchase, and encouraging Friends to watch over the morals of the slaves they already had.

But the matter would not be put to rest and came up again and again in the yearly meeting sessions. Gradually, Friends consciences were tendered, and each time they moved farther toward the freedom of the slaves. In 1776, a committee was appointed to assist Friends throughout the state in manumitting slaves, and in 1778 North Carolina Yearly Meeting issued an order against all buying and selling of slaves by Quakers. As early as 1775, the yearly meeting had directed that local monthly meetings should disown members who refused to take steps to free their slaves.

To encourage compliance with yearly meeting directives, that body appointed a committee to visit local meetings and assist

Friends to free their slaves. Not all were as tender as Thomas Newby and his friends, nor as compliant as Obadiah Harris and Jesse Henley. There were those who argued that the blacks would be unable to care for themselves and that slavery was in their best interest. However, if these Friends continued to resist the committee over a period of time, their monthly meetings disowned them.

IV

CAESAR AND GOD

I Joseph Jordan... being fully persuaded that freedom is the natural right of all mankind....
— *Manumission Paper, 1826.*

In all this, the North Carolina Yearly Meeting followed a steady course once it had established a policy of condemning slavery. Manumissions increased, and gradually Friends cleansed themselves of the curse of owning slaves. Yet, the State of North Carolina kept up its struggle to defend the institution. Not only were the slaves freed by Quakers picked up and resold, but new laws were passed restricting manumissions. The yearly meeting, to protect manumitted slaves, appointed their former owners as guardians. As the United States became a reality after the Revolutionary War, it was still theoretically possible to free slaves for meritorious service, as it had been under British law; some were so liberated, but the courts were harsh with Quakers. For example, when our old friend Thomas Newby sought to free a black girl named Nacy (or Nancy?) in 1787, he described her virtues generously, and then added that he was "clearly convinced in [my] mind that it is wrong for me to hold her as a slave." That was enough to cause the court to deny the request. To free an African–American hero for sentimental reasons might be possible but to suggest that holding a slave was wrong could not be tolerated. The courts knew very well that Quakers were really in favor of freeing *all* slaves.[27]

After 1791, a slaveholder was required to post bond for each slave freed. The amount was set by the courts and varied from one hundred pounds to as much as a thousand. When slaves were freed, they were supposed to leave the state within a year. Nevertheless, it is clear that this requirement was not strictly enforced, because there were many free blacks living in the state permanently. The requirement appears, rather, to have been used for blackmail in case a black person's freedom was challenged, and, specifically, it was used to harass Quakers.

Yet Quakers kept on freeing their slaves. They prepared manumission papers like the one issued by Joseph Jordan for Moses, Sarah, Sam, Cuts, Rachel and her child, and George, in 1826. That document is preserved for us and reads as follows:

> I Joseph Jordan of Northampton County in North Carolina From Mature Deliberate Consideration of the Conviction of my own mind being fully persuaded that freedom is the Natural Right of all mankind, and that no Law moral or Divine, has given me a just Right of Property in the persons of any of my fellow Creatures, and being desirous to fulfill the Injunction of our Lord and Saviour Jesus Christ by doing to Others as I would be done by, do therefore declare that having under my care a Number of Negroes Named and aged as followeth, Moses aged near forty one years, Sarah aged near thirty seven, Sam aged near twenty nine years, Cuts [illegible] aged near twenty five years, Rachel aged seventeen years and her child, George aged eleven years, Patience aged near eight years, Charles aged five years, David aged two years, Silas aged near four months, I do myself my heirs exd. and Administrators, hereby Releas unto as many of them as are come of age of Twenty one, women Eighteen, all my Right Interest and Claim or pertensions of

Claim whatsoever as to their persons or to any Estate they may hereafter acquire, and those now under age to partake of the same Privilege Liberty and Estate as they come to the ages above written, without any Interruption from me or any person Claiming for, by from, or, under me, in witness whereof I have hereunto Set my hand and Seal this tenth day of the Eight Month in the year of our Lord one thousand Seven hundred and Eighty four.

Sealed and Delivered in the Presence of Samuel Parker, Aaron Lancaster. (Signature and seal, Joseph Jordan)[28]

When the freedom of liberated slaves was threatened the yearly meeting hired lawyers to protect them. Many such records appear in county records of the time.

The immediate reason for the Quaker manumissions was the conviction that slavery was a sin and that every Quaker must cleanse his soul of this sin. Joseph Jordan said he had to free his slaves because he wanted to "fulfil the Injunction of our Lord and Savior Jesus Christ by doing to Others as I would be done by." Yet there was more to it than that. In the same document Jordan says that he is "fully persuaded that freedom is the Natural Right of all mankind and that no Law moral or Divine has given me a just Right of Property in the persons of my fellow Creatures." This makes the matter more than a purely personal one or even a sectarian matter. "Natural Right" and "moral and Divine Law" are universal terms and apply to everyone. They are also the language of the Constitu-

On the opposite page, a photocopy of the Joseph Jordan manumission paper of 1784. Friends Historical Collection, Guilford College.

I Joseph Jordan of Northampton County in North Carolina From Mature Deliberate Consideration of the Convictions of of my Own Mind, being fully persuaded that freedom is the Natural Right of all mankind and that no Law moral or Divine has given me any Just Right to or Property in the persons of any of my fellow Creatures, and being Desirous to fulfill the Injunction of our Lord and Saviour Jesus Christ by doing to Others as I would be done by, do therefore declare that having under my Care a Number of Negroes Named & aged as followeth, Moses aged near Forty One Years, Sarah aged near Thirty Seven Years, Sam aged near Twenty nine Years, Cedo aged near Twenty five Years, Rachel aged near Seventeen Years, the Child George aged near Eleven Years, Patience aged near Eight Years, Charles aged near five years, David aged near two years, Silas aged near four Months, I do for myself my heirs Ex.rs & Administrators, hereby Release unto as many of them as are come of age men Twenty one, Women Eighteen, all my Right Interest and Claim or pertentions of Claim whatsoever as to their persons or to any Estate they may hereafter Acquire, and those now under age to partake of the Same Privilege Liberty & Estate as they Come to the ages as above Written, without any Interruption from me or any person Claiming for, by, from, or, under me, In witing Whereof I Have hereunto Set my hand and Seal this tenth Day of the Eighth Month in the year of our Lord One thousand Seven hundred and Eighty four ——

Sealed & Delivered
in the Presence of
Samuel Parker
Aaron Lancaster

Joseph Jordan (Seal)

tion. A petition to the North Carolina State Legislature by the North Carolina Yearly Meeting of Friends in 1788 insisted that laws prohibiting the freedom of slaves were "in no wise consistent with the principles of the Established Constitution & contrary to the Declaration of Independence of the United States of America." In another petition of 1790, restrictions against emancipation were declared to be contrary to the duty they [the Quakers] owed "to the Invincible Father of all the families of the Earth." This again is universal language and not limited to the borders of the Religious Society of Friends or even to Christendom.

V

QUAKER FREE NEGROES

A distinguished Catholic lawyer in the service of Truth.

By 1808, matters had reached an impasse. Large numbers of black people had been freed by Quakers; yet they were unfree because their former owners continued to be responsible for them, and if they strayed their freedom was threatened by the police and the courts. What could be done?

In this extremity, the Quakers turned to a friend who had already helped them in the courts: He was Judge William Gaston, a humane and honorable lawyer who deplored slavery. He was the son of a Huguenot refugee who had fled Catholic France, went first to England, and then settled in America. Here, he met and married a woman who happened to be a Catholic, and so it came about that their son William was reared a Catholic. Catholics were regarded with suspicion in North Carolina and, indeed, throughout much of America at that time, so young William knew a kind of religious persecution himself. Later, when he became a lawyer, he was instrumental in winning the right of Catholics to hold state office, which before had been the exclusive privilege of Protestant Christians. He wrote and spoke courageously, if discreetly, about the evils of slavery.

To meet the dilemma which the Quakers faced, he made a novel proposal: Let the North Carolina Yearly Meeting of Friends become the owner of the freed slaves. The courts had ruled that slaves were property and not legal persons before the law, and

Judge William Gaston.
Photo reprinted with permission of the Greensboro Historical Museum.

churches were authorized to hold property. Wealthy slaveholders often gave slaves as gifts to churches so they could hire them out as a source of income. This being the case, argued Gaston, the yearly meeting, as a church, had a perfect right to take legal title to slaves.

Of course, explained Judge Gaston, these persons would not be treated as slaves. They would be paid wages, would not be separated from their families, and would be given freedom as soon as the law allowed. If anyone tried to steal them or mistreat them, the yearly meeting would use its agents and hire lawyers to protect them.[29]

This proved to be a popular idea, and one after another of the Quakers deeded their "slaves" to the yearly meeting. When this became known, some non–Quakers who opposed slavery, also freed their slaves and gave them to the yearly meeting. Indeed, so many did so that the time came when Friends said they could no longer receive assignments from non–Quakers. By 1814, the agents of the yearly meeting reported that most of the slaves still technically owned by Quakers had been assigned to the yearly meeting.

Persons so freed came to be called Quaker Free Negroes. To deal with the heavy responsibility of the care of the Quaker Free Negroes, the yearly meeting created the Meeting for Sufferings.

VI

BACK TO AFRICA. HAITI.

Many of them were eager to go to the land of their forefathers.

And still the legislature held out against freedom. At the North Carolina Yearly Meeting in 1824 the decision was made to offer freedom to the former slaves held by the yearly meeting by sending them to the new Republic of Haiti. That tiny country was just emerging from devastating wars which had brought it freedom from France. It was the first black republic in the world and sought to make itself a model of freedom and opportunity. It was also seriously depopulated by the terrible wars. The new government offered land grants and gratuities to settlers who would till the soil.

In eastern North Carolina enthusiasm for the new plan was such that, in November of 1825, the Eastern Quarterly Meeting reported to the Meeting for Sufferings that it had already sent 506 persons to Haiti. In 1826, there was a carefully planned Quaker expedition sailing from Beaufort, North Carolina, on the good ship *Sally Ann*. By now the freed slaves under the care of Friends were commonly called Quaker Free Negroes, and 119 of them boarded the freedom ship. Friends Phineas Nixon and John Fellow helped gather the emigrants from as far away as Deep River in Guilford County, and went with them to Haiti. They docked in Aux Cayes on July 6, 1826. When the Friends agents returned, they reported a friendly reception and satisfactory arrangements for housing and jobs.

Emigration to Haiti went on in some form for at least six years. There were conflicting reports about how the emigrants were faring. Quaker Thomas Kennedy accompanied another group on the *Sally Ann,* and in his group was an ex-slave named Samuel Radcliff. Although Kennedy reported that he found some of the previous emigrants well established, he found others "unpleasantly situated." On the other hand, Radcliff's assessment was more optimistic. In a letter to Thomas Kennedy, he said that he was saving money and making plans to go back to North Carolina and purchase the freedom of his two children and take them back to Haiti with him. He had found freedom in Haiti preferable to slavery in North Carolina.

Nevertheless, Haiti gradually lost its appeal. Unfavorable reports kept filtering back, and the news spread in the black community. Just how strong the feeling became is illustrated in a story told to the author by the late Hugh Moore, a native of eastern North Carolina, who reported in 1981 that it was still repeated among Quakers in that area. According to this story, a very large black man, a Quaker Free Negro, confronted his Quaker guardian with a rumor that he

Quaker Free Negro refuses to go to Haiti.

was to be sent to Haiti. This so enraged the man that he threw the Quaker to the ground and held him there until he promised not to send him to Haiti. The agents of the yearly meeting had, of course, been instructed not to send anyone against his will, but obviously some blacks felt pressure. The unhappy saga of Haiti continues. As this is written, in 1992, 2,160 Haitian refugees fleeing their homeland and headed for Florida have been picked up by the United States Coast Guard with the intention of returning them to Haiti. A judge in Miami has issued a temporary restraining order, but Florida is already a refuge for thousands of Haitians who have fled political and economic troubles in that unhappy island. Quakers made an unfortunate choice 150 years ago.

In the search for a suitable home for their charges, North Carolina Friends also turned to Liberia. Liberia, the "land of liberty," was a colony established on the west coast of Africa by the American Colonization Society as a home for freed slaves. Because some of the earliest black persons sent there were captured and resold into slavery, Congress authorized the American Navy to stand guard off the coast of Liberia to intercept any attempt at such kidnapping. The project reflected a view held by many white Americans that African–Americans should be "sent back to Africa" to escape slavery and oppression in this country. Many good people thought it would be the best solution. Even Abraham Lincoln asked his secretary of the Navy to estimate how many ships would be required to send the entire black population to Africa. The story goes that he was informed that if the entire American Navy were so employed, it would be unable to carry even the *increase* in population, so that the black population would keep on growing regardless.

Nevertheless, North Carolina Friends saw it as a way to get their own charges to freedom. It was an expensive undertaking, and more funds were needed. They, therefore, turned to their own affluent

Quaker Free Negroes board ship for Liberia in Norfolk, VA.
Engraving. Picture Collection, The Branch Libraries, New York Public Library.

and solidly antislavery Friends in Philadelphia for help. Friends there responded generously, but expressed a preference for sending the Quaker Free Negroes to free states in the United States.

The Liberia project grew into a very large undertaking. The American Colonizaion Society, which managed it, was in chronic need of money, so Friends were enlisted to raise funds. Recruitment for the ships sailing from Norfolk, Virginia, went on all across the state and was conducted by agents of the Meeting for Sufferings of North Carolina Yearly Meeting. Some of their charges were eager to "go back to Africa," although none of them, of course, had ever been there. The very first settlers to go under the Colonization Society settled on the small island of Sherbro just off the coast of present Liberia. There, many perished from disease and the strange climate, but gradually a beachhead was established on the mainland and a viable colony was set up. Between 1827 and 1831, North Carolina Friends sent many of their ex-slaves to that colony. There must be a great many people in the Republic of Liberia today who are descended from Quaker Free Negroes from North Carolina.

Three ships known to have carried North Carolinians to Liberia merit attention: The *Doris*, the *Nautilus*, and the *American*. The brig *Doris* took Quaker Free Negroes to Liberia at least three times. In 1826, Quaker Josiah Parker reported from Eastern Quarterly Meeting to the Meeting for Sufferings at Jamestown that he had delivered forty-one of his own charges to Norfolk to board the brig *Doris*. Many of them, he said, were eager to go "to the land of their forefathers." He explained that the Quaker women took great bolts of cloth, bought especially for this purpose, cut out, and made a new outfit of clothing for each of the forty-one emigrants.

The trip to Norfolk, Virginia, from eastern North Carolina was made in two rented wagons. It was winter, it was cold, and it rained incessantly. The roads turned into a sea of mud and the trip was delayed, but when the wagons finally got to Norfolk, the brig *Doris* had not yet come in. Friend Josiah located a big house for his charges to stay in while they waited.

Enemies of colonization frequently charged that planters used the relocation plan to get rid of their old and infirm slaves, but this was clearly not the case with this group of Quaker Free Negroes. Josiah Parker tells us that those he placed in the big house in Norfolk consisted of only one person over sixty, a third children under twelve, and the remainder between the ages of fifteen and fifty-two.

The wait for the brig *Doris* wore on. It was cold and rained and rained, and the overcrowding and idleness got on everyone's nerves. Was it for this that they had left their secure homes on the Quaker plantations? Besides, the people of Norfolk, both white and black, began to make fun of them for wanting to leave America for the primitive life of Africa.

While the group in Norfolk waited for their ship to come in, word came that thirty-two more Quaker Free Negroes were coming on the canal from North Carolina but that their barge had stalled when the canal froze over. John Kennedy, the dedicated Friend from Wayne County, North Carolina, who also represented the American Colonization Society, sent two covered wagons from Norfolk to pick them up. The horses splashed through the mud on their rescue mission.

Meantime, Quaker Aaron White and his wife arrived from North Carolina to see the ex-slaves off on their passage to Liberia,

Liberia-bound Quaker Free Negroes from North Carolina abandon barge frozen in a canal.

but when they heard about the people stranded on the frozen canal they turned around and went back to help. They said they wanted to make sure the stranded passengers were handled gently as they were transferred to the wagons.

By January 24, the new arrivals raised the total of Quaker-held blacks headed for Liberia to eighty-four. And still, the *Doris* had not come. By February 1, they were still waiting, but on March 19, John McPhail of the Colonization Society wrote: "After the Doris sailed...."

The miserable experience in Norfolk discouraged further emigration to Liberia, but then word came back that the *Doris* had arrived safely, and the mood changed. In Jamestown, Nathan Mendenhall received word that the emigrants were delighted with their tropical paradise and were busy in agricultural pursuits. Two small children had died on the passage to Liberia, but at the time that was considered a modest loss on such a hazardous journey.

The good news from Liberia encouraged others to go. The *Nautilus* sailed on December 16, 1827, with 142 persons for whom Quakers were responsible. The Meeting for Sufferings paid $1,132.48 3/4 for "outfits and embarkation" for these persons.

Nevertheless, interest in Liberia was now waning. In July, 1828, Caleb White requested that the Meeting for Sufferings not send any more recruiters for Liberia into the Eastern Quarter.[30]

VII

THE MANUMISSION SOCIETY. BRIDGES.

Doing to others as they would be done by.

With opposition to slavery accepted as a fixed tenet of Quaker thinking in North Carolina, a variety of efforts were undertaken to further the antislavery cause. It was soon clear that freeing themselves of the sin of slaveholding was not possible without political action. Quakers also recognized the need to convince others of the fundamental conflict between the love of freedom professed in the new republic and the denial of freedom inherent in slavery. One effort to form a bridge between Quakers and other antislavery forces was to organize the Manumission Society.

In 1816, a Quaker minister and abolitionist named Charles Osborne came over the mountains from Tennessee to organize the North Carolina Manumission Society. Actually, Osborne was from an old–line Quaker family of Centre Meeting in Guilford County, North Carolina. It was, quite naturally, at Centre Meeting that he assembled a group of persons to organize the Manumission Society of North Carolina. It was not limited to Quakers. The first act of business was to name a committee to solicit the support of other major religious denominations. They went two by two and came back from the general assemblies of those churches with favorable responses from the Presbyterians and Moravians. Such visits continued.

This organization did many interesting things in its short life, for it lasted only fifteen years. They made a survey which indicated that sixty percent of the general population favored emancipation. They were able to get their antislavery message before the public through *The Greensboro Patriot*, which was edited by William Swaim, himself an abolitionist and descended from a family of Nantucket Quakers.

*William Swaim, abolitionist.
Reprinted with permission of the Greensboro Historical Museum.*

The Manumission Society also sent antislavery petitions to the legislature paralleling those of the North Carolina Yearly Meeting of Friends. In both cases, nothing came of the petitions, for the slaveholding forces were determined not to allow general manumission. The society was in contact with other groups in other states, and in 1826 it was announced that there were one hundred manumission societies in the United States, forty-five of them in North Carolina. At its height, it was estimated that there were more than two thousand members in North Carolina. In addition to the "regular" societies composed of men, there were several Female Branches in North Carolina, one of them at Jamestown.

The Manumission Society had wide appeal among non-Quakers as well as Quakers. Benjamin Lundy, a famous advocate of the cause and editor of the *Genius of Universal Emancipation*, reported that he had spoken to a crowd at a militia muster in North Carolina and observed that it was a curious mix of people in Quaker garb and military uniforms. At one point, a crowd of 300 gathered on the banks of the Yadkin River and formed a chapter of the Manumission Society. An amazed onlooker reported: "There was not a Quaker among them."[31] Nevertheless, the last meeting was held at the Marlborough Friends Meeting in 1834, and the African-American population of North Carolina was still in bondage.

Actually, there had been some reason to believe that the restrictions on freeing slaves might be lifted. There were members of the legislature who opposed slavery, and there was usually somebody willing to introduce bills in support of the Quakers, even if they were always defeated. When Quakers were made guardians of the slaves they freed, it was always with the thought that the laws would soon change so that manumitted slaves could live as free persons. Yet, the years went by and no progress was made. Even worse, from time to time laws were passed reinforcing slavery.[32]

VIII

Quakers In Court

When Quakers hold slaves, nothing but the name is wanting to render it at once a complete emancipation.
— *Chief Justice Taylor of the North Carolina Supreme Court, 1827*

Quakers of the nineteenth century were reluctant to go to court on general principle. Matters should be worked out amicably among Friends through the monthly meeting, and with other persons they should strive to live in peace. However, slave matters brought North Carolina Friends into court frequently as they tried to manumit their own slaves and protect them from recapture. When the yearly meeting became owner of the so-called Quaker Free Negroes, dealing with the courts became a necessity. This was due in part to the very nature of the plan prepared by Judge Gaston: Were the Quakers *really* the owners of these former slaves? When the matter finally reached the State Supreme Court in 1827, Judge J. Ruffin argued that, since owning slaves violated the religious principles of the Quakers, it was impossible for them to own them. Furthermore, he said, allowing them to work for wages meant that they were not really slaves and had already been manumitted in violation of North Carolina law.

Quakers did not deny their opposition to slavery. They declared openly that they were holding their charges only until the slaves could be legally freed in North Carolina or, failing that, could be removed to another state. As a church, they held that they had a right to hold slave property. The legal situation was blurred, and Quakers felt that they were defying an unjust law.

Two bodies, then, were on a collision course: Quakers were determined to see slave laws altered so they could free their slaves and live under the law in good conscience, and the legislature of North Carolina was determined to hold the line against any change in the laws which would threaten the institution of slavery.

The Quaker policy, then, had to be to work for a change in the laws and, at the same time, to look for ways to remove their charges to places where they might enjoy their freedom if it continued to be impossible in North Carolina. We have cited the efforts to change the laws: repeated petitions to the legislature, lobbying in Raleigh, working through the Manumission Society, and assorted efforts to affect public opinion in the state. In point of fact, Richard Mendenhall, a key figure in the Meeting for Sufferings and active in all the work to free and protect slaves, was himself a member of the legislature. So was his brother, George C. Mendenhall, an "accidental" slaveholder, disowned by Quakers for holding slaves received through marriage. But George C. Mendenhall was a lawyer and helpful to Friends in their antislavery work. Yet, the legislature would not be moved.

Not only did Friends have the care of slaves assigned to them by Friends in 1808, but their number increased year by year. Their care became a matter of much labor and some controversy. In the east, where slaves were numerous, membership in the Friends meetings was in steady decline because of heavy emigration to the western states. The eastern agents, living over 200 miles from Jamestown where the yearly meeting's Meeting for Sufferings was headquartered, tended to act on their own. Both in east and west, the Quaker-held blacks were hired out and a part of their earnings withheld for their maintenance, with another part held in escrow

Gaston's elegant sophistry that the yearly meeting was a *bona fide* owner of slaves, but the work did not end. Perhaps they were encouraged by Associate Judge John Hall's dissent in the case. He commented on "our unfortunate connection with slavery," and spoke with appreciation of the "sentiments of humanity" entertained by the Quakers. The policy from that time seems to have been that the trustees as individuals took assignment of slaves, with the private understanding that they would continue to earn wages and either be manumitted or sent out of the state as soon as possible. The Meeting for Sufferings actually continued its work very much as before.

Joe

In 1825, Friend Asa Folger was conducting a group of Quaker Free Negroes to Indiana by way of Kentucky when one of his charges named Joe (often spelled Jo) was kidnapped. He reported the crime to local authorities, but they were not satisfied from the evidence that Joe was really a free man. Asa sent an urgent message to Jamestown for Joe's papers so he could go into court in Grant County, Kentucky, to get him freed from the kidnapper. George C. Mendenhall, acting for the Meeting for Sufferings, took the matter up with his friend, Congressman Romulous M. Saunders, who in turn approached Colonel Richard M. Johnson, a congressman from Kentucky. When the authorities in Kentucky received an authenticated bill of sale for Joe, and learned of his powerful friends, it was enough to liberate him from the extortioner who held him — and into the security of the local jail. As soon as word got to Asa Folger, he went back to Kentucky from Indiana to claim Joe's freedom and take him to safety on free soil. Mindful of the danger, he took Joe in the best Underground Railroad fashion to freedom across the Ohio River into Ohio. One might well suppose that this was the end of the episode, but it was not to be. As soon as he was on free soil, Joe revealed a secret he had been holding from his benefactor: He had fallen in love with a woman in Kentucky. Indeed, while he was being held by the kidnapper, he married the woman, and his heart was heavy because he had left her behind. The matter was complicated by the fact that his new wife was a slave, but he loved her so much that he wanted to go back to Kentucky and work out redemption.

Poor Asa's elation at freeing a slave turned to desperation. He had just experienced the hostility toward free slaves in Kentucky and knew at first hand how complicated it was to get redress in the courts. If Joe went back to Kentucky, he would be a marked man and would almost certainly be forced back into slavery in a few days. There would be no chance to earn enough money to redeem his wife. Confronted with these difficulties, Joe asked Asa for a loan to redeem his wife and bring her to freedom in Ohio or Indiana. Considering the hazards involved, Asa felt unable to do this on his own and wrote Nathan Mendenhall for advice. Mendenhall felt the

Joe longs for slave bride he left behind in Kentucky.

matter was beyond resolution and wrote to Asa that it seemed to him "he is out of the reach and direction of our meeting." At this point we lose track of this story of a love that was so great it was willing to risk slavery rather than abandon the beloved.[35]

Newlin v. Freeman

Between 1839 and 1849 a curious situation arose at Saxapahaw, North Carolina, within the limits of Spring Monthly Meeting. John Newlin, a member of Spring Meeting and an active member of the Meeting for Sufferings, owned a cotton mill at Saxapahaw, and in that mill he had a group of slaves at work — or at least that is what people thought. For one hundred years members of the Newlin family pondered the strange contradiction that a Quaker of such solid credentials would own slaves.

As it turns out, John Newlin did not own slaves, and the black people working in his mill were Quaker Free Negroes working for wages. A widow named Sarah Freeman (Friedman) died in 1839, and when her will was probated it became known that she had left her slaves to "Newlin," that is, John Newlin of Spring Meeting. She stated that she and her husband had always intended to send their slaves to a free state. But when they found out that "she could not do that," she determined to leave them "to some steady old Quaker, who would not own slaves." That steady old Quaker was John Newlin.[36]

All this was deeply disturbing to the heirs of Sarah Freeman. They entered suit to overthrow the will, but Newlin and the Meeting for Sufferings managed to maintain the technical ownership of the slaves until the matter was finally settled in favor of the Quakers in 1849. There was a proviso in the court decision, however, which required Newlin to emancipate the slaves "in accordance with the statute of 1830," which required a bond of $1,000 for each slave and their removal from the state in ninety days. Of interest in the case is the fact that the Freemans were of

German origin and Sarah was unable to read English.

Court records testify to the long legal battles of North Carolina Quakers to free, or maintain the freedom, of slaves. In 1810, Quakers sued for the freedom of two black children in Beaufort, North Carolina, whose mother was a free black. In Greensboro in 1817–1820, they gained the freedom of Benjamin Benson, a free black who had been kidnapped in Delaware and sold as a slave in Guilford County. In 1818, they undertook the defense of a mulatto girl named Penny who was under the care of Exum Newlin. She was said to be freeborn, but efforts were being made to reduce her to slavery. In Guilford County Thomas Wright left five slaves to New Garden Meeting in his will so they could be given their freedom, but his widow sued for their possession. The case wore on for fifteen years, from 1816 to 1831, and was finally settled in favor of the Wright estate.

These few examples illustrate clearly that North Carolina Friends were seen as defenders of the freedom of African–Americans in general, not only those who had come to them through inheritance or assignment. A measure of this public perception appears in the case of a black girl named Mary whose freedom was threatened in Carteret County in 1851. Her mother was a free black woman. Mary's freedom was confirmed by the court through intervention by the Quakers. James Davis, who handled the case, wrote to the Meeting for Sufferings that there was great public interest in the case. "The slaveholders" he wrote, "were afraid I would gain her freedom and the cry of abolitionist was heard in the streets." Obviously, the word abolitionist was a fighting word in North Carolina at the time.[37]

The courts often reflected a sense of humanity, along with a determination to administer the laws. When Mary's mother Hannah was threatened with slavery by the same person claiming Mary as a slave, the judge ruled for her freedom and lectured the claimant.

He said: "...after a period of thirty years, the defendant, without a pretense of right, as far as we are informed, seized upon the plaintiff and questions her right to freedom....After so long an acquiescence by the public in her enjoyment of her freedom, every presumption is to be made in favor of her actual emancipation, especially against a trespasser and wrong–doer."[38]

Much has been written about the climate of opinion in the South, and specifically in North Carolina, during the nineteenth century. Judges were often sympathetic to slaves; yet Quakers lost hard–fought cases. Efforts of the Quakers and the Manumission Society would seem to indicate that manumission was virtually impossible; yet the superior courts granted several hundred manumissions each year. Sometimes the General Assembly granted individual manumissions. In Fayetteville in 1833, fifty–five white citizens signed a petition to the legislature for the freedom of one David Sutherland and his wife. In general, the legislature reflected widespread interest on the part of the public in reducing the burden placed upon the slave, but it drew a hard line against anything that might threaten the institution of slavery itself.

This policy is seen in the rejection of a petition made by Quaker Caleb Winslow for the freedom of his slave Mills in 1816. The petition is vague in describing the required "meritorious service" of Mills, but the real motive of the petitioner came out clearly enough when Caleb declared that as a Christian he felt compelled to "do to others as I would be done by." Such an attitude denied the very basis of slavery, and the petition was rejected.[39]

We have already observed that Quakers suffered from a serious generation gap in the slave matter. Sons and daughters did not automatically share the antislavery sentiments of their parents. Indeed, the most common threat to the freedom of Quaker–held Negroes was from the heirs of Quakers who had either fallen away from the Quaker faith or were disowned for any of a number of reasons. Disownment was often for slaveholding, although marrying out of meeting or living a corrupt or immoral life were also common reasons. While Quakers were the first organized religious group in the state, membership in the Society of Friends dwindled as the nineteenth century wore on.

Harriet Peck, a Rhode Island Quaker teacher in the New Garden Boarding School in 1837, described a back–slidden Quaker in a letter to a friend. Harriet was an abolitionist and a member of an abolitionist society in Rhode Island, so she was alert to what was going on around her. One person she got acquainted with was a certain "Dr. Mendenhall" who had grown up as a Quaker in Guilford County. He had even been active in antislavery work in his youth, he said. Later, he married a non–Friend in South Carolina and became a member of the Baptist Church, even becoming a Baptist preacher. When he talked with Harriet, he was the owner of quite a few slaves, explaining that people had no respect for a white person who didn't own slaves.

Over against the gloomy picture we have painted about the attitudes toward slavery by some ex–Quakers, we must point out also that many others retained their testimony to the worth of all races after they left their Friends meetings. There was George C. Mendenhall who was disowned because he married out of meeting and thereby acquired slaves. Yet, he continued to represent Quakers as a lawyer and actively supported manumission. After his first wife died, he married Delphina Gardner, an antislavery activist. He freed his slaves in his will. William Swaim, the editor of the *Greensboro Patriot*, and Jonathan Worth, governor of North Carolina, symbolize the continuing influence of the Quaker testimonies in families who no longer held membership with Friends. Charles A. Beard, the historian, was the grandson of a North Carolina Quaker who had been disowned for marrying out of meeting, but he was a member of the Manumission Society and moved his family to the free state of Indiana. There, he sent his children to Quaker schools.

Hindsight tells us clearly enough that the long struggles of North Carolina Quakers in the courts did not bring an end to slavery. Of course, this was not the object of the court action, but rather the elimination of injustices under the law. Yet, the dialogue in these cases did point the way toward a society in which all would be free. At the same time Quakers petitioned untiringly for the end of slavery. The progress made in civil rights in the United States after 1964 rested on an indispensable law, the Civil Rights Act of 1964; yet the actual gaining of these rights often has come only as individual cases came to court. What was lacking in the period we are considering was specific legislation guaranteeing the rights promised so grandly in the constitution. Quoting the "all men are created equal" and "general welfare" phrases from the constitution as Quakers and other manumissionists did was not enough.

Despite all their efforts, North Carolina Quakers found the institution of slavery intact in 1848 when the Meeting for Sufferings made its final report declaring its mission accomplished. Slaves held by Quakers were at last free in other states and countries.

As for the Quakers themselves, their numbers had been decimated by emigration to the West, and those remaining had lost much of their zeal for bringing the curse of slavery to an end. What they had done was to wash their hands of it. The limited goal set for itself by the Meeting for Sufferings is described in the final report of that body in 1848. The neatly printed report was entitled *A Narrative of Some of the Proceedings of North Carolina Yearly Meeting on the Subject of Slavery Within its Limits*.[40]

In a strictly technical sense, the mission had been accomplished. But there were some Friends in North Carolina who felt it was not enough for Quakers to have relieved their own consciences by gaining freedom for the slaves owned by themselves and their forbears. They were still living within a slave society, and they could not feel at ease until slavery itself was ended. They brought it up year after year at yearly meeting, and it was clearly an embarrassment to the Quaker establishment. Daniel Worth, the ex-Quaker become a Wesleyan Methodist antislavery activist in Indiana, accused North Carolina Friends of having become a sham and a prop of "the infernal institution." His charge seems justified by the astonishing Epistle of Advice issued by the North Carolina Yearly Meeting in 1843. It declared:

> Whereas it is a well known testimony of the society of friends that they do not allow their members to hold slaves or in any way to interfere with the system of slavery further than by petition, reason and remonstrance in a peaceable manner; and it having through report come to the body of the society that some one or more of the members thereof have suffered themselves to be so far overcome through sympathy to allow and give shelter improperly to one or more slaves and thus occasioned several of our fellow members to be accused of like improper conduct. We have therefore thought it due to ourselves and to the people at large in the country in which we live thus to make known our long established practice and utter disapproval of such interference in any way whatever while at the same time we do not in the least degree relinquish our testimony to the injustice of slavery.[41]

This amazing epistle reflects a widespread reaction to the increasingly militant abolitionist movement. It was a loud and vigorous campaign carried by newspapers, lecture halls, and churches, orchestrated against the background of an ever more active Underground Railroad. The issue was increasingly drawn in bold black and white, dividing the nation into two camps. There was even some division among northern Quakers who had labored long and hard against slavery, when it began to appear that the issue might well lead to war. In New York Yearly Meeting, George F. White even praised a fugitive slave for returning to his master, declaring, "I had a thousand times rather be a slave and spend my days with slaveholders than to dwell in companionship with abolitionists." In the South, the newly formed Methodist Episcopal Church South announced "the broad and explicit disavowal of the Methodist Episcopal Church of any right, wish or intention to interfere, in any way, with the relation of master and slave, as it exists in the slaveholding states of the union...."[42]

But from other quarters came another message. Quakers, North and South and in different ways, held to their conviction that slavery was wrong; they differed on ways to end it. Gradualists still hoped that increased manumissions and new laws would bring about the end of slavery. North Carolina Yearly Meeting was forced to clarify this point in 1844, attempting to make amends, it seems, for the harsh epistle of 1843. It issued a letter to the monthly meetings urging Friends to work against the evil of slavery in such ways as they could "in good conscience."

IX

THE JULIUS PRINGLE

Freedom is due a person in the land where Providence gave him birth.
— *Josiah Forster, English Friend*

At a time when it seemed there would be no more Quaker Free Negroes going to Liberia, history intervened in a way that no one could have foreseen. We know that the slaveholding establishment always feared a slave insurrection. This fear had grown at the time of the terrible violence in Haiti, which had culminated in the independence of the colony from France and the establishment of the black Republic of Haiti. There was also the disturbing Denmark Vesey "insurrection" in Charleston, South Carolina, in 1822. But in 1831, there was a very real — and very terrifying — incident in Southampton, Virginia, just across the Dismal Swamp from the large Quaker settlements in North Carolina.

Nat Turner, a slave on a Southampton plantation, was a talented preacher and leader among the slaves. In due course, he came under the conviction that, like Moses of old, he had been appointed by God to liberate his people from slavery. At an appointed hour he and his followers murdered the owner of the plantation where Turner lived and roamed through the countryside massacring white people. In all, fifty-five people were killed. The revolt was quickly crushed by overwhelming forces, and thirteen slaves and three free blacks were hanged. Turner himself was captured and hanged. It was the most serious slave insurrection in American history.

This incident was a serious blow to the work of North Carolina Quakers. The effect was immediate and dramatic. Thirty blacks were jailed in Duplin County, North Carolina, twenty-five in Sampson County, and fifteen in New Hanover. Two were hanged in Onslow County, and about fifteen were lynched by white mobs in the eastern part of the state. New restrictions were placed on the movements of slaves. Every slave had to have a pass to step off his master's plantation. There was panic in both black and white communities.

At that time, in Core Sound, North Carolina, Quaker Jonas Mace found himself in charge of "forty or fifty" ex-slaves who technically belonged to the yearly meeting. It was a time when they certainly needed all the protection they could get. With the option of refuge in Haiti and Liberia virtually ended, Friend Jonas reported that most of his charges had said they would be willing to go to one of the western states. But there was trouble there too. An emissary from Indiana had come to North Carolina to report strong anti-black feeling in that state, and he urged that no more of the Quaker Free Negroes be sent there. He even said that there was a new law against bringing more blacks to Indiana, although at this moment in history it was no more than a rumor.

With the uproar about the Nat Turner Rebellion, the Quaker-held blacks desperately wanted to leave the South. It all caught Jonas Mace at a bad time. In a letter to the Meeting for Sufferings, he complained that he had been put to so much trouble and expense with the Quaker Free Negroes that he was very weary and eager to get the matter settled. He had hoped they might be willing to go to Haiti. As he was pondering his next step, word came that the ex-slaves had decided they would go to Haiti after all, just to escape the imminent danger in North Carolina. At least, that is what Jonas Mace reported to Jamestown on May 20, 1832. On June 3, *Benjamin* Mace sent a passenger list of ninety-two persons who were bound for Haiti on the schooner *Julius Pringle*.

Yet, on the same day the *Julius Pringle* was reported bound for Haiti, George Swaim reported to Nathan Mendenhall in Jamestown that ninety blacks departed for Philadelphia on the *Julius Pringle*. In any case, it is clear that the *Julius Pringle* did go to Philadelphia with its cargo of refugees.

Now, Philadelphia, the City of Brotherly Love, had been receiving freed slaves and runaway slaves for some time. When Quakers took their charges to that city, they were met by Philadelphia Quakers who helped them get settled and get jobs. But recently a backlash had developed in Philadelphia. It was said that there were too many blacks in Philadelphia already, and even some Quakers complained that some of those who had come had earned a poor reputation in that city.

The matter reached serious proportions when James Peale arrived in Philadelphia with a group of Quaker-held blacks from North Carolina, only a short time before the *Julius Pringle* arrived, and no one was willing to receive them. Feeling ran so high that an angry mob formed, and it was only when Philadelphia Quaker Benjamin Cooper stepped forward with an offer to be personally responsible for the good conduct of the refugees that the mob finally dissolved.

When the news spread that the *Julius Pringle* was en route to Philadelphia with a shipload of black refugees from North Carolina, the old fears began to stir again. George Swaim rushed to the city to receive the ship, but Friends there told him that, if it docked there, there would be a new Boston Tea Party. Into the midst of this storm came an innocent David White, still another agent of the Meeting for Sufferings of North Carolina Yearly Meeting, with fourteen additional Quaker Free Negroes.

There was panic in the city and among Philadelphia Friends as well. As always in tense moments, rumors exceeded the facts. The number of people aboard the *Julius Pringle* rose from ninety-two to 600. Instead of peaceable persons brought up by Quakers to be moral and nonviolent, they were said to be the very persons who had roamed the countryside slaughtering white people in Southampton County, Virginia.

Slowly, the ship entered the mouth of the Delaware River, passed New Castle, Wilmington, and Chester, and finally did dock in Philadelphia, in spite of the threats. Then, there was a standoff. The atmosphere in the city was so charged that the passengers were not allowed to leave the ship. It was June 14, and the weather was unbearably hot. For three days the hapless refugees fleeing slavery and the threat of death in North Carolina endured the heat and frustrations of their cramped quarters, and endured the hostility and threats of a great northern city. Some of them begged to go back to North Carolina. It was suggested that they might go to Liberia, but remembering the tales of hardship there, few of them wanted to go.

Finally, after three days of agony in Philadelphia Harbor, Friends in that city located a farm at Red Bank, New Jersey, that was willing to receive them. At that place they were finally able to leave their cramped quarters — but their final destination was still unsettled. Now, a committee of five Friends from the Chester-Philadelphia area set about finding a solution for the refugees. First, they reopened the question of Liberia. Returning to North Carolina in the shadow of the Nat Turner Rebellion seemed foolhardy, and Philadelphia was now out of the question. Haiti was increasingly unattractive and apparently had already been rejected. The committee then contacted the American Colonization Society, which agreed right away to provide passage to Liberia. The wandering pilgrims gradually decided that, of all the alternatives, Liberia was probably the best. Only one woman chose to stay "near the

Delaware" and one small child died, but the remaining eighty-eight agreed to go to Liberia.

Now, Pennsylvania Friends set about doing what North Carolina Friends had been doing for some years: they outfitted the black émigrés for the trip to a new home. The first step was to divide the group into "households" — ten of them, and each "family" was provided with household utensils: pots and pans, skillets, knives, tableware, etc. Since most of them would be agricultural workers, they were given axes, spades, shovels, and hoes. Some were carpenters, bricklayers, plasterers, blacksmiths, turn-

*Philadelphia crowd demonstrates against
black refugees from North Carolina*

ers, and shoemakers. These also were provided with the tools of their trade: hammers and saws for the carpenters; trowels for the bricklayers; trowels, hammers, and forges for the blacksmiths; lathes for the turners; and lasts, knives, and hammers for the shoemakers. These lists also provide us with an interesting look at the training that these persons had received from their Quaker masters.

One of the things the Friends were careful to do was to be concerned for the moral and spiritual welfare of the émigrés. They gave them Bibles, school books, and religious tracts, and counseled them on the importance of "avoiding the use of *ardent spirits*, and of maintaining a sound moral reputation, as well as contributing to the support of suitable associations for divine worship."

On balance, Pennsylvania–New Jersey Friends got a much more favorable impression of these people than had the frightened non–Quaker citizens of Philadelphia. They described them as "orderly, temperate, industrious, and intelligent...likely to advance the interests and general prosperity of the colony."

By the twelfth of July, the party was ready to board the brig *American* for the journey to Africa. Two trusted men went with them, for there were still fearful stories of ships being diverted from the route to Liberia and landing instead in New Orleans, where the free blacks were sold into slavery. It was reassuring, then, that the captain of the *American* was the same William Abels, a Methodist minister, who had captained the *Julius Pringle* from North Carolina to Philadelphia. Another trusted person on the passage to Africa was Joseph Robertson, who had been in charge of the group on the *Julius Pringle*, and whom Philadelphia Friends had hired to go with them to Liberia. To reassure them still further, Jonas Mace, the Quaker who had started them on their way from North Carolina, met the ship when it put in at Norfolk, Virginia. He comforted them and wished them Godspeed as they headed out for the South

Atlantic on the long journey to Africa. The *American* arrived in Mesurado, Liberia, on September 13, 1832, three months and ten days after the group had embarked on the *Julius Pringle* in North Carolina for Philadelphia.

Jonas Mace waves farewell to Quaker Free Negroes en route to Liberia.

Even though there had been a lot of reluctance about going to Liberia, the report came back that they had been well received there. *The Friend*, a Quaker journal published in Philadelphia, carried this story on December 7, 1832:

> The company was well received by the governor and other officers of the colony. Each family was settled in a comfortable house, with the understanding that they were to have the privilege of

occupying it for six months, if they inclined to do so. Daily rations of rice, and other articles of good and wholesome provisions, are served out to each family, which it is understood, will be continued for six months if required; this supply, the agents learned from one of the emigrants, is so abundant as to enable some of the most provident of them to make occasional savings over and above their actual daily wants. Orders were given by the governor for an allotment, in fee simple, of a farm of ten acres of land, also a lot of half an acre in the TOWN, to each family.

From the best observation our agent was capable of making, every able bodied emigrant might obtain immediate employment at liberal wages — the mechanics [say] from $1.50 to $2.00, and labourers 75 cents to $1.00 per day.

Some of them expressed an intention of writing home encouragement to their friends to follow them to the colony.[43]

The North Carolina Quakers who had labored to get the *Julius Pringle* group to Philadelphia, and finally to Liberia, gave a great sigh of relief when the news of the safe arrival came. George Swaim wrote a long letter to Nathan and Richard Mendenhall of the Meeting for Sufferings in Jamestown, summarizing the whole affair. He recounted how he had spent many years in this type of work trying to "do to others as [he] would be done by." In doing so, he had neglected his own business affairs to the extreme that before he left for Philadelphia on his mission to protect the Quaker Free Negroes, he had had to persuade the sheriff to postpone judgment against his house for $750.00. Benjamin Mace was tired too. He said that most of his relatives had already migrated to the

West, and as soon as he could get his affairs in order he was going to follow them.

Apparently a few of the Quaker-held Negroes were still going to Liberia on American Colonization Society ships sailing out of Norfolk, but by 1836 David White reported to the Meeting for Sufferings that those remaining flatly refused to go. It was not only that some emigrants sent back discouraging reports from Liberia despite the glowing article of 1832, but the whole atmosphere of the antislavery movement was changing. Even as early as 1817, a convention of free blacks in Philadelphia declared that it would oppose anything that would "have a tendency to banish us from [America's] bosom." Such resettlement was described as cruel and "in direct violation of those principles which have been the boast of this republic."[44] Also, abolitionist sentiment was growing among whites, especially in the North. Instead of freeing slaves gradually through manumission or resettlement, they insisted that they should all be freed at once through legislation or decree. Such sentiment began to reduce contributions to the Colonization Society. Among the heavy supporters of colonization were the Tappan brothers, who had made a fortune in the drygoods business. In 1833, the Tappans announced that they were switching their contributions to the abolitionist movement.

North Carolina Friends were being urged to embrace the abolitionist cause. London Yearly Meeting, which had always been held in such high regard by North Carolina Friends, now was encouraging American Friends to embrace abolitionism. There was lively correspondence between Josiah Forster, clerk of London Yearly Meeting, and Jeremiah Hubbard, of the North Carolina Meeting for Sufferings. Josiah argued that the American black man was no more an African than a white man was an Englishman or other European. By the same logic, he said, white Americans, as Europeans, should be sent "back to Europe," leaving the country to the Indians, its rightful owners. In a memorable phrase, he said that freedom is due a person "in the land where Providence gave him birth." Jeremiah, himself, one-fourth Cherokee, argued back that whites and blacks found themselves in very peculiar circumstances in America, which made manumission a proper policy for American Friends. Nevertheless, Josiah's logic influenced thinking among Friends in North Carolina. He also travelled to America and propagated his views widely.

Abolitionist sentiment spilled back to North Carolina from other parts of America, as well as from England. In 1831, Indiana Yearly Meeting of Friends instructed its Meeting for Sufferings to communicate with other yearly meetings, encouraging them to call on the General Government to abolish slavery in the United States. In 1838, North Carolina Yearly Meeting itself petitioned the state legislature to "legislate for the extermination of slavery in this state."

Colonization in Liberia and Haiti was now at an end, but there were still free blacks under the care of Friends in North Carolina, and the legislature still refused to relax the obstacles to manumission. Abolitionism was so out of favor in North Carolina at that time that few dared speak in favor of it. Even abolitionist literature was prohibited, and certainly every effort was made to keep it out of the hands of slaves. In these circumstances, North Carolina Friends returned to their original decision to resettle their charges in free states within the United States. Even that was not without problems, as the hostility of Philadelphia made clear in the *Julius Pringle* episode.

X

RESETTLEMENT IN OTHER STATES

The above ground railroad.

The colonization of Quaker Free Negroes was not a part of the original plan of North Carolina Friends. The purpose of the Meeting for Sufferings and the Gaston Plan was simply to hold and protect them until such time as they could be freed in North Carolina or sent to some "free government." George C. Mendenhall stated in his will that his freed slaves should go to "some State or Government where slavery is not tolerated or allowed by law."[45] This movement to the free states had begun before the colonization venture and diminished only when problems began to appear in those states. A committee had been appointed in 1823 to look into the laws of Ohio, Indiana and Illinois.

Although the groups going overseas were quite large, those going by land were usually small. Those going under the care of Friends were all carefully accounted for and prepared for the journey. A list was drawn up giving the ages of the emigrants, their former owners, manumission papers if they had them, and any other information that might be needed. The "conductors" who were in charge of the expeditions were given powers of attorney to dispose of the slave "property" in the free states. As in the case of those going overseas, each emigrant was given a new outfit of clothing made by Quaker women from bolts of cloth bought for that purpose. It was warm clothing suitable for the colder climates in the North and West. These groups traveled by wagon, and horses and wagons were bought specifically for that purpose. This was an open "Above Ground Railroad" that required no false bottoms or other subterfuge. Since the trip to Richmond, Indiana, a common destination, was given as 481 miles, it was common to sell the horses and wagons there instead of bringing them back empty. There were two main routes for this traffic, one from Hertford to Greensboro and on to Richmond–Newport, Indiana, by way of Kentucky and Cincinnati. The other (more common one) went from Greensboro north to Fincastle, Virginia, and across present West Virginia to Gallipolis, Ohio, and from there to Richmond–Newport. (See map p. 70.) Another spur took some free blacks to the Quaker settlement at Mt. Pleasant, Ohio, near Pittsburgh. In any case, the moment an expedition crossed the Ohio River it had reached free territory.

Given the plodding gate of heavy horse–drawn wagons over a primitive mountain road, this was a very long trek. New Garden–Greensboro was a gathering point for the expeditions going west, and reports from that period speak of as much as six weeks for the trip.

Young Friends caravan conducts slaves to freedom in Indiana.

As Quakers began to free their slaves and less cotton was raised, many planters suffered hard times and began to emigrate westward. The Meeting for Sufferings took advantage of this movement to get small groups of African–Americans to free territory. In 1826, Thomas Kennedy wrote to Nathan Mendenhall that they were "about getting some of [their] black people to the State of Indiana," and inquired if anyone from Jamestown–New Garden was moving to that state and would be willing to take some of them along. This was only one of what must have been many such instances.[46] As early as 1814, the Meeting for Sufferings reported that forty black persons had been sent to freedom in Philadelphia, and small groups and individuals went from time to time.

The organized groups under the direct sponsorship of the Meeting for Sufferings, provide the names of individuals who were the "conductors" of these expeditions. They appear in the minutes and correspondence of that body. One of these was Asa Folger, who conducted a group to Indiana by way of Kentucky in 1825 and had in his company the famous Joe. Folger was a member of the Manumission Society. Then there was the case of Joseph Hunt. In 1826 and 1827, he took two groups of black persons to Clinton County, Ohio, a place belonging to Indiana Yearly Meeting. It was a time of increasing opposition to bringing freed slaves to Ohio and Indiana, but the Committee on African Concerns of Indiana Yearly Meeting sent a formal receipt to the North Carolina Meeting for Sufferings listing the names of persons for whom Joseph Hunt had power of attorney. A special committee was appointed to "advise and assist said persons of colour in procuring places of residence, getting employment, and such other aid as may be necessary."[47]

David White is worthy of special attention. Not only did he lead emigrant groups, but he also made arrangements for others and was active in defending black persons in court when their freedom was threatened. Perhaps one of his most exciting moments was

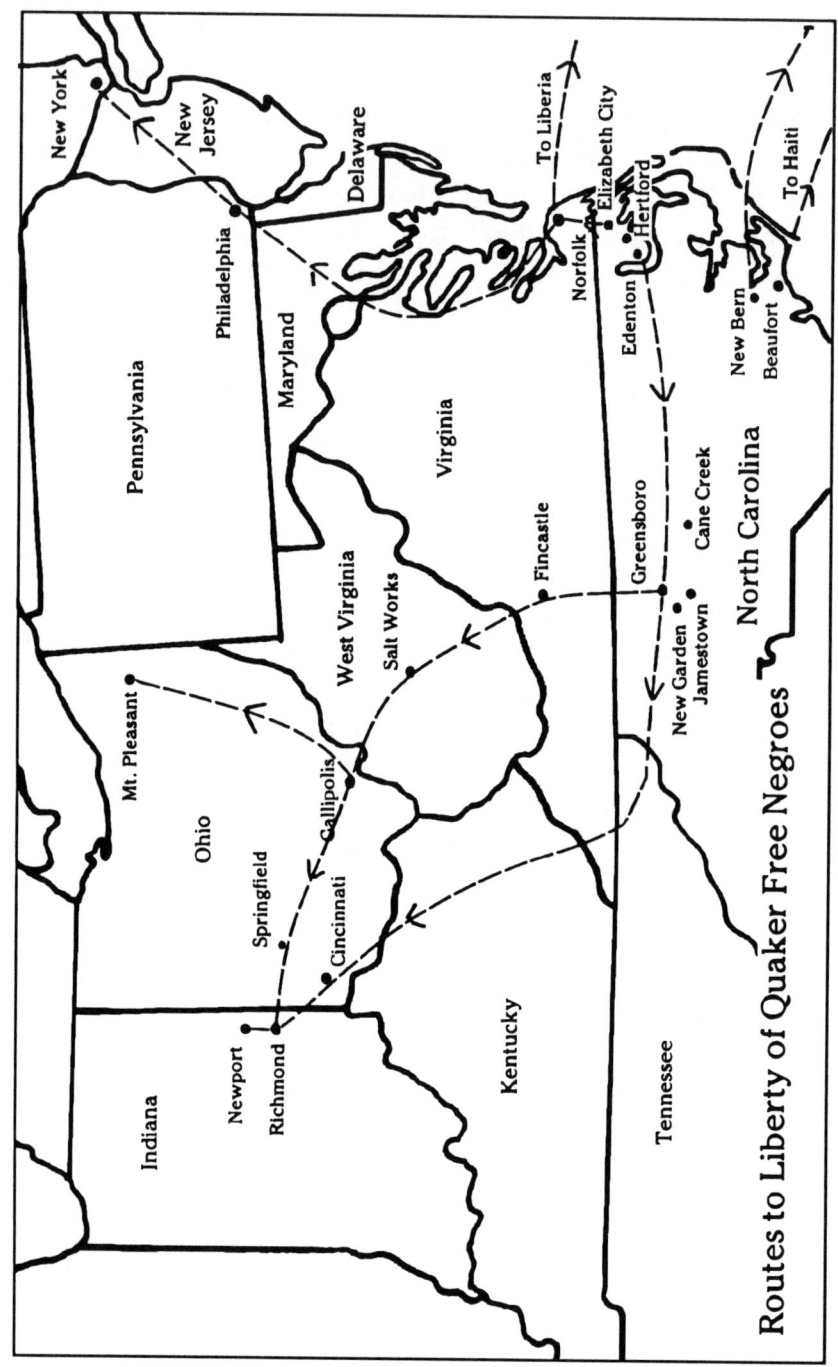

when he arrived in Philadelphia in 1832 with thirteen charges from North Carolina at the very time when the unwelcome ship *Julius Pringle* was lying at anchor there and was not permitted to unload its cargo of human refugees. Three years later, he took fifty-three Quaker-held blacks to Indiana, and the next year he was back in Philadelphia again. That time he managed to leave only one refugee in the City of Brotherly Love, but New York Friends gave a friendly welcome to the twenty-seven others he had brought with him.

One of the most ambitious expeditions was carried out by Young Friends in 1834. The trustees of Eastern Quarter bought twelve horses and thirteen wagons for that expedition at a cost of $2,490. The cost was so great that some of the trustees borrowed money on their own collateral to finance it. It was a virtual caravan. Two groups of fifty-three and thirty-five got off on October 10, and the final group of forty-five left on October 15. The Young Friends carried powers of attorney "to manumit, set free, settle or bind them out." For this expedition of 133 souls we have the names of Robert Peele, Thomas Outland, and Miles White as conductors, but obviously it was a much larger group.

XI

The Underground Railroad

All those laws admitting the right of slavery are, before God, NULL and VOID.
— *The Anti–Slavery Society*

Certainly Levi and Addison Coffin were proceeding "in good conscience" when they aided runaway slaves in the Underground Railroad. Both insisted that they did nothing to persuade the slaves to run away, but eagerly responded to those who were running away from abusive masters, or who found they could no longer endure bondage. Knowing this, runaway slaves sought them out. Addison Coffin says that most Friends in North Carolina were reluctant to take part in this work of liberation themselves, but as Quakers they were willing to contribute money and help out in such ways as they could "in good conscience."

Since aiding runaway slaves in the South (and in the North under the fugitive slave laws) was illegal, there are no hard statistics of the number of people who were active in the Underground Railroad, or shielded runaways in their homes. The slaveholders themselves claimed that 100,000 slaves deserted them between 1810 and 1850, and Ohio emancipationists boasted that they alone had helped 40,000 blacks escape. Such claims caused great nervousness among slaveholders, which increased whenever there was a slave revolt anywhere, whether in Virginia's Nat Turner Massacre of 1831, or anywhere in the Caribbean or South America. The reaction was always to impose new restrictions and increase repression.

One thing that spurred people like Levi Coffin to become antislavery activists was the traffic of Virginia slaves across the state on their way to the lower South. Levi wrote of his anguish as a child when he saw slaves in chains on this doleful trek. Slaves always dreaded being "sold south" because of the severe treatment they were said to suffer there. In any case, to be sold was to risk exchanging a reasonable and benign master for a cruel one. Billy Proctor, a Georgia slave, wrote to a Mr. Lamar begging him to buy him for $1,000. "I am fearful that if you do not buy me," he wrote, "there is no telling where I may have to go."[48]

Levi and Katie Coffin

The defenders of slavery were especially troubled by the effect of "subversive literature." Enemies of freedom often become book burners. One of the books that most troubled slaveholders in North Carolina was Hinton Rowan Helper's *The Impending Crisis*. Adding insult to injury, Helper was himself a native of North Carolina and knew about slavery first hand. From up North, he beckoned the black man to come up North and harshly condemned the slaveholder. When Daniel Worth came to North Carolina in 1859 with his fifty copies of *The Impending Crisis* in his luggage, ownership of the book was forbidden; consequently, the distribution of the book had to be done cautiously to avoid the attention of the authorities.

In this connection, there is an amusing story about Nereus Mendenhall, principal of the New Garden Boarding School near Greensboro, through the Civil War years. Mendenhall owned this forbidden book and word of it came to the authorities in Greensboro. Officers went to New Garden to arrest him, but when they got there and searched the premises they failed to find the offending book. It seems that his good wife had advance notice of the search and burned the book. When they asked her about the book, she answered that there was no such book in the house. Certainly, many others read this hard-hitting exposé of slavery. One of them was William Mendenhall, to whom a copy was inscribed in 1860. It is preserved in the Guilford College Library.

Pressure for emancipation continued to grow in the northern states and in England. British Friends expressed their deep concern about slavery in their annual epistles to North Carolina Friends. In 1853, they even sent a commission to the United States with a minute of concern for the abolition of slavery and delivered it personally to the president and to the governors of several states.

In Boston, William Lloyd Garrison published the flamboyant *Liberator* under a masthead which warned slaveholders with these words: "Your covenant with death shall be annulled and your agreement with Hell shall not stand." The Anti-Slavery Society operated under a resolution adopted in 1837 that declared that "all those laws...admitting the right of slavery are, before God, NULL AND VOID."

Such fire–breathing language was not in the mold of the gentler strain of Quakers. Even that great challenger of slavery, John Woolman, admits in an essay that there might be circumstances under which a benevolent and just slaveholder could be within the will of God.[49]

The militant antislavery wing of North Carolina Quakers shared the views of their co–religionist, John Greenleaf Whittier, and the abolitionists of the North to a large extent. There could be no compromise with slavery. They offended their more conservative friends by using subterfuge and trickery when necessary to help fugitives. Levi Coffin's *Reminiscences* are filled with such stories. There was the time that Levi found himself in Virginia talking to a North Carolinian who told him he was looking for a runaway slave named Jack Barnes. Levi pretended to be sympathetic to the plight of the slaveholder and offered to help him find his "property." He then proceeded to get the man well drunk in the tavern before he went out looking for the slave. When he found him, of course, he warned him to get away as fast as he could. By the time his owner sobered up, Jack Barnes was well on his way to freedom on the Underground Railroad.

The Underground Railroad itself was a wide–ranging understanding, rather than a formal organization, stretching west all across the slave empire. There were known havens in the homes of sympathetic persons, some Quaker, some not. When possible, such "stations" were located about twenty miles apart, a distance which a slave could reasonably be expected to travel in a night. There seems to be truth in the story that they followed the North Star on clear nights. On cloudy nights, they might be directed by moss on the north side of trees, or by nails driven into a post, stump, or prominent tree whenever they reached a fork in the road. On the route from North Carolina north, some of the nails were probably driven by the Coffins. Levi boasted that he had walked the whole 500 miles from North Carolina to Indiana three times.

When the fugitives came to a river, they followed the instructions for making a raft. Lifting a few rails from a nearby fence they lashed them together with vines being careful not to use wire or nails. To do so would have been to leave evidence of the trail. They then floated their crude craft in the river and paddled across with their hands. Once there, they cut the vines with a knife and allowed the loose rails to float down the river. When some passing farmer noticed the rails the next day, he concluded that some mischievous boys had thrown some rails into the river as a prank.

The southern terminus of a busy route of the Underground Railroad was New Garden, North Carolina, where New Garden Meeting, New Garden Boarding School, and Levi Coffin's family were located. The story of Arch Curry comes from this place. A free black woman named Vina was a washerwoman at New Garden Boarding School, and she was married to a free black named Arch Curry. It was necessary at the time for free blacks to carry manumission papers or other proof that they were not slaves. Even in northern states, slave-catchers picked up African-Americans without papers and returned them to their masters in the South. This was technically against the law until the Fugitive Slave Act made it legal. At length, Arch Curry died, leaving Vina a widow and in possession of Arch's manumission papers. She decided to loan these to male slaves bearing some resemblance to her late husband, so they could travel north safely. The lucky man would travel to Newport, Indiana, with his false papers, where he would hand them to Levi Coffin. From there, he could pick up the Underground Railroad network and go on to Canada. For his part, Levi Coffin gave Arch Curry's papers to a trusted courier who took them back to Vina at New Garden, North Carolina. Vina then gave the papers to another slave yearning to be free, and the whole process was repeated. No one knows how many slaves won freedom on Arch Curry's papers.

Quakers and others protected slaves who were being pursued by their masters. Levi Coffin wrote about a slave woman named Ede who came to the Coffin house in North Carolina at night with her baby in her arms and her heart full of terror. She had just learned that her master, Dr. David Caldwell, was going to give her as a gift to his daughter who lived 100 miles away. The daughter's husband was a Presbyterian minister. The thing that especially disturbed Ede was that she would be separated from her baby. She pleaded for help from the Coffins.

The Coffins took her in and comforted her, even though, as Levi tells us, his father was subject to a fine and imprisonment for harboring a runaway slave. Dr. Caldwell, the owner of Ede, was an eminent citizen, a physician and educator, who is still remembered and honored in Greensboro. He had a fine library, and Levi Coffin got most of his education reading books loaned him by David Caldwell. Given this close personal relationship, Levi decided to go to Dr. Caldwell personally and plead Ede's case. The good Dr. Caldwell, slaveholder that he was, listened sympathetically to the young Quaker and decided to allow Ede to stay in the household with her baby.[50]

Family traditions in the present generation of Quakers in North Carolina bear witness to the aid given to the movement by families in the state. Dorothy Teague Pollet writes from Siler City of the work of her great grandfather Needham Perkins. He was a Quaker minister living in Pikeville, North Carolina, and had been a teacher in New Garden Boarding School. Fernando Cartland gives important space to Perkins in his *Southern Heroes*. Dorothy Pollet writes: "Many, many times my mother, Octavia Hockett Teague, used to tell us about Great Grandfather helping the slaves to run away. In the winter he always kept a roaring fire and the slaves would rest on the big rug before the fire. In the morning they were always gone."

In Jamestown, North Carolina, was the Mendenhall Inn. The resident proprietor was Richard Mendenhall, the tireless antislavery activist through his work with the Meeting for Sufferings and the Manumission Society. He was also a member of the state legislature. North Carolina Yearly Meeting, in what would seem to be a cruel and vengeful act, appointed him to a committee to circulate the astonishing Epistle of Advice of 1843 condemning the harboring of runaway slaves. Yet, when he died in 1851, a memorial prepared for him stated rather pointedly that in his home "The stranger ever found a friend and the wayward traveller needed only the tattered badge of poverty to secure him a place where 'to lay his head.' The widow and the orphan were never turned away." Was this a veiled reference to the harboring of runaway slaves? Local and family tradition insist that his home-inn was a station on the Underground Railroad. Mendenhall Inn is a museum today, and the official line is that this was such a haven. Among the antiques on display is a wagon with a false bottom used to spirit slaves to free territory — although this wagon came to the display from another Quaker home.

The home and inn of Richard Mendenhall in Jamestown, North Carolina.

Slaves were not the only fugitives sometimes harbored by Quakers. Generations of Americans grew up singing about "John Brown's Body" without having any idea who he was. This John Brown, an ardent antislavery activist, won notoriety by leading a posse that "executed" five pro-slavery leaders in Kansas. Although a fugitive from the law, he became a hero of the abolitionists. Later, he was executed by federal authorities following an armed insurrection at Harper's Ferry, Virginia. John Brown had been an anonymous guest in the home of Quaker Henry Copeland at Rich Square Meeting in Northampton County, North Carolina, during 1857. His daughter, Julia Copeland Outland, said that her father "never turned a stranger away," and Brown spent ten days in the Copeland home without revealing his identity. It was only when he was executed two years later and it was national news that the Copelands learned whom they had entertained.[51]

Sometimes Quaker antislavery activists in North Carolina were the object of bitter hostility by slaveholders. Among those who received verbal abuse was Isham Cox. Cox was a member of the Meeting for Sufferings and a sympathizer of the work of Daniel Worth. An anonymous person identifying himself only as "A Slaveholder," wrote him a threatening letter sometime between 1857 and 1859. He accused him of being a friend of Daniel Worth and even allowing him to "hold prayer in your family." Among his evil deeds, according to the letter, was that he was helping to circulate the pernicious "Helper's Books." The letter concluded:

> Now, sir, if the institutions of our country do not suit you why do you not remove to Ohio or Indiana where this evil does not exist? You may rely that the public eye is on you and I would advise you to pursue a prudent and persistent course of conduct and let Vestal and Worth take care of themselves. You will have to change your course in order to

satisfy the public that you are a good citizen and a law abiding man.[52]

Friends in North Carolina, during this period, faced a cruel dilemma: Could they be law–abiding citizens, as they wished to be, and yet remain faithful to their conviction that slavery was wrong? Judge Gaston had helped them by establishing the elegant subterfuge that allowed the yearly meeting to "own" slaves, thus freeing the individual conscience. For half a century, Friends tried continuously to bring about a change in the laws so that they would not have to resort to subterfuge. Powerful forces among them had concluded that they must live in the midst of slavery for a very long time, and, in the struggle between conscience and the law, they chose to live in peace under the law. Other Friends, led by the Coffins and such persons as Isham Cox, acted under the banner of the Anti–Slavery Society: "All those laws admitting the right of slavery are, before God, NULL AND VOID." They proceeded to violate the law whenever required to free the slave and did it in good conscience, because they believed they were obeying a higher law. And all the while, a great stream of Quakers who were convinced that the dilemma was insoluble on North Carolina soil pulled up stakes and resettled in the West.

Levi Coffin is remembered in Greensboro, NC.

XII

The Civil War

He was a true patriot, he loved his country, his whole country, this glorious Union.
— A tribute to George C. Mendenhall by his widow, Delphina Gardner Mendenhall, 1860.

The Civil War did not come as a complete surprise. There had been rumblings of secession for some time, and the militance of the antislavery forces of the North reached such a high pitch that many had concluded that war was inevitable. After all, the United States was still a young country. Anyone older than seventy–five might still remember George Washington, who died in 1799. An eighty year–old person would have been eighteen when Washington was inaugurated for his first term as president. President Lincoln himself remarked at Gettysburg that the Civil War was a test to see whether a nation dedicated to the proposition that all men are created equal could "long endure." There was still some doubt that it could. Several republics within the Soviet Union recently seceded from that union after a lapse of time similar to the secession efforts of the southern states in America.

For the Quakers of North Carolina, it was a severe trial. Not only were they opposed to all war, but they certainly were not willing to fight for the preservation of slavery, which they had opposed consistently for a century. Already in 1860, at the yearly meeting held at the old meeting house at New Garden, there was a special joint session of the men's and women's meetings to consider the "commotions" then troubling the nation. It was a solemn meeting for worship and prayer that God "would turn the hearts of rulers and people, to righteousness, justice and mercy, and that our present form of Civil government, with all its attendant blessings, may be preserved in peace, and all be overruled to his glory."

The Minute of Advice going out from the 1861 yearly meeting expressed the grief of Friends at the turn of events:

> This is a time of peculiar trial; but let none be discouraged. As our country becomes more and more distracted and torn by strife, let us as a people unite more closely together. Though iniquity abound, let not our love wax cold, but rather increase, till, like Abraham, we may be prepared to make any sacrifice which may be called for at our hands.[53]

The trials of war were not long in coming. Since so many Quakers had already emigrated to the West (i.e., Indiana, Ohio, Illinois, Iowa, and Kansas), some families chose the time of crisis to join their relatives there. When it became a trend, the authorities turned them back when possible. Draft–age Quaker men often hid out in the woods or made their way over the mountains, or northward, to Union territory. But it was not only Quaker young men. Others who opposed slavery, or were Unionists, or pacifists, also fled the South. This very fact meant that the authorities tried by every means to conscript every able–bodied young man into military service to meet the demands of the Confederate government.

Such vigorous recruiting caused the yearly meeting to redouble its efforts to gain exemption from military service for its young men. There had been a tradition of such exemptions for Friends in North Carolina since the time of the British colonial governors, going all the way back to Archdale, the Quaker governor, in 1695. The State of North Carolina had confirmed the exemption. The Confederacy, on the other hand, was a new creation and it required new negotiations. John Carter and Nereus Mendenhall travelled to the Confederate capital at Richmond, Virginia, in 1861, to plead for exemption from the secretary of war. They were unsuccessful, but in 1862 the Confederate Congress did establish a $500 exemption fee, which many paid, but others refused. Finally, in 1864, the assistant secretary of war gave approval for certain kinds of work as alternate service. One was at the salt works at Wilmington, North Carolina, where conditions were said to be terrible. Some refused to do any kind of alternate service on the grounds that it contributed indirectly to the war effort. Others worked in industries owned by Quakers, such as the tanning and shoe industries of Allen U. Tomlinson in Springfield. Throughout the war, there was a certain amount of harassment of young Quaker men, because it was assumed that they were loyal to the United States and in favor of universal emancipation.[54]

In truth, this assumption was usually correct. Those who fled across the mountains to go west were not only opposed to slavery, but were usually opposed to secession. Allen U. Tomlinson was often in Richmond to plead the cause of North Carolina Friends before the Confederate War Department and the Confederate Congress. Quaker John B. Crenshaw, a resident of Richmond, was a tireless agent of North Carolina Friends in that city. Fernando Cartland quotes from Crenshaw's diary for the year 1864 in his well-known *Southern Heroes*. On 4th month 12th of that year, Crenshaw says that he had to get a pass to go home, and then goes on to say, "We all renewed our allegiance to the United States." On 4th month 26th, he records that he "went with Allen U. Tomlinson to affirm his allegiance to the United States. Got a pass to go home." Often this involved no duplicity, because there were those living within the Confederacy who argued quite openly that the Union cause was the just one.

Actually, North Carolina had been reluctant to embrace secession. Although slaveholding forces were very powerful, controlled the legislature, and intimidated the press, only 24 percent of the white population actually owned slaves, according to some estimates; others said fewer. In the so-called "Quaker congressional district," Randolph County voted 2,446 to 45 against even holding a convention to consider secession in 1861.[55]

Seeing that Quakers were standing firm in their rejection of both war and slavery, quite a few non–Quakers were attracted to them. Patrick Sowle says in an article in *Quaker History* that as many as 600 came voluntarily seeking membership because they shared the convictions of Friends. Non–Friends, with not a little malice, called them War Quakers, and the name stuck. Some of them had grown up in Friends families and not bothered to formalize their membership, while others came to these convictions through study of the Bible and inner struggle. It is said that not one of the War Quakers relented, although a few birthright Quakers did so. At least one War Quaker, Seth Laughlin, died in the Confederate prison at Windsor, Virginia, as a result of abuse.[56]

Fernando Cartland has given us a long list of Friends who suffered abuse and of others who refused to serve in the Confederate forces. One thing that emerges is that the real enemy was war itself, which so inflamed the passions of the people that some of them did things that they would not have done under normal circumstances. The sadistic practices attributed to some persons, usually young men, were generally performed by zealots on their own account. Often, superior officers or higher Confederate officials deplored such practices and tried to prevent them.

One frequent problem was that the Exemption Act of 1862

applied only to those who had joined Friends before the act was passed, but there were many who joined later. In such cases, the authorities sometimes accepted an assurance from the yearly meeting that these persons were sincere pacifists. In the case of some fifty who refused to pay the exemption fee, the yearly meeting paid. Sometimes, the yearly meeting was permitted to certify that a non–Quaker was a sincere conscientious objector.

Yet, it should not be supposed that Quakers had an easy time of it in the South during the Civil War. It was a time of real suffering, not only for those eligible for military service, but also for farmers, whose farms were raided and often completely ruined by both contending armies as they took what they needed to feed their men and horses.

One of those who suffered much for his faith was Thomas Kennedy, the same person we have already seen engaged in the work of liberating slaves long before the war came. His father before him was a wealthy man and a slaveholder, but on his deathbed he had willed his slaves to the yearly meeting, which, in turn, had sent them to Africa. Thomas, himself, received about eighty slaves whom he personally accompanied to Haiti and liberated there, according to local historians.[57] Through trickery, Thomas was convicted of treason by the Confederate authorities and sent to the infamous prison at Salisbury, North Carolina. He was 66 years old at the time. He received such abusive treatment at Salisbury, and later at a prison in Richmond, Virginia, that, when he finally arrived in Indiana through a prisoner exchange, he died within a few days in the home of Friends.

A handwritten account of the sufferings of Levi Hollowell Massey is kept in a family Bible by members of the Massey family.[58] The principle source of such accounts continues to be Fernando Cartland's *Southern Heroes*, published in 1895. Recent interest in local history is bringing other cases and further details to light.

The spiritual blight of owning slaves haunted North Carolina Quakers right down to the moment of the Civil War. As late as 1859, the yearly meeting minutes tell of "one or two instances of owning by heirship" and, in 1860, two by heirship. This does not take into account the peculiar circumstances of the estate of George C. Mendenhall and his widow.

George C. Mendenhall was a member of the distinguished Mendenhall family of Jamestown. Indeed, Jamestown was named for his grandfather, James Mendenhall. George C. Mendenhall who established a law school, Telmont, in Jamestown (now under the High Point reservoir), was a state senator and disowned Quaker. The disownment came about as a result of his marriage to Eliza Dunn, a non–Friend who owned slaves. As a slaveholder, and for marrying out of unity, he was disowned. Yet, George C. Mendenhall remained loyal to Friends principles, served the Meeting for Sufferings on slave matters, and steered the charter for the New Garden Boarding School through the state legislature.

Sally Stockard, a local historian, is our authority for the special policy that George C. Mendenhall set for his slaves. She tells us that he operated a large "industrial labor farm, that the slaves were taught trades, there were Negro clerks in his store who sold and bought goods, there was a harness shop kept by a slave, and one of his slaves was a carpenter who helped build the capitol in Raleigh. When President Buchanan visited Chapel Hill, George C. Mendenhall sent his caterer to wait on him. Mendenhall's will tells us that he was an immensely wealthy man, with real estate holdings in several counties in North Carolina, as well as in five other states."[59]

A son, James Ruffin, was born to George C. Mendenhall and Eliza Dunn Mendenhall, and then Eliza died. Subsequently, Mendenhall married Delphina Gardner, daughter of Barzilla Gardner, an ardent antislavery activist. Delphina was no less committed to the freedom of the slave than her father; indeed, the freedom of the slave was her consuming passion.

What followed was an interesting pact between George C. Mendenhall and Delphina. For the rest of their lives together they collaborated on ways to free their slaves. Since they had both been active in the legal removal of blacks from the South, they chose this method for the Mendenhall slaves. But there was not enough time to accomplish this task in George C. Mendenhall's lifetime. In 1859, he willed his remaining slaves to Delphina, and within a year he died.

The will, as probated in Guilford County in 1860, gives specific instructions to his executrix, Delphina Mendenhall, in the following words:

> It is my will that all my slaves male and female of every description and by whatever name and all their increase and descendants after the date of this will shall be emancipated from slavery (this not to interfere with those which are conveyed in deed and in trust to Thomas C. Dunn) in a manner prescribed by the laws of North Carolina — and that provision be made out of my estate for their removal out of this State and for them to be located in some other State or Government where slavery is not tolerated or allowed by law and for all my slaves to enjoy their freedom and my Executrix is hereby directed to take all lawful ways and means necessary for emancipating all said slaves.[60]

The wording of the will expresses well the views not only of the Mendenhalls but also of North Carolina Yearly Meeting: Emancipation and procedure within the law. Mendenhall's earnestness is reflected in his provision that the work of removing and freeing the slaves is to take precedence over all other claims on his estate.

In a letter to Cyrus Mendenhall in March of 1860 Delphina paid high tribute to her late husband and confirmed the views of many Quakers and other North Carolinians as well. She said he was a "true patriot — He loved his country — his whole country — This glorious Union....Yet the sympathies of his heart...went out to the remotest tribes of earth and he is not ashamed to own a reverence for the very lowest form of humanity." She adds that he wrote a letter to his friend the Hon. T. Nelson congressman from Tennessee to congratulate him on his "beautiful national oration." In the context of the times she says that he was deeply disturbed by the talk of secession.

The death of her husband placed Delphina in a great dilemma: She, the great advocate of freedom for the slaves, was now a slaveholder. It was to bring her much trouble — and opportunity.

Delphina Mendenhall was a many-faceted woman. She wrote poetry and corresponded with the great Quaker poet, John Greenleaf Whittier. The *Friends Review*, published in Richmond, Virginia, published some of her poetry. One of her unpublished poems describes the adventure of accompanying some of her slaves over the mountains to free territory:

> Slowly rolled our heavy wagon
> Slowly fell our lingering footsteps —
> Though our wheels rolled on toward freedom
>   Thus each step unbound a chain —
>
> Carolina! Carolina!
> Joy and [?] grief were strangely blending
> Tears of sadness, tears of gladness
> In our tearful, wordless farewell,
>   We can never meet again!

> Through Virginia's lonely forests,
> Up her lofty steps ascending,
> We have reached her towering summits,
> > We have crossed the crystal streams;
>
> We have rested on her bosom,
> We have coiled [?] within her shadows,
> We have warmed beneath the radiance,
> > Of her summer's golden beams.
>
> We have pitched our tents at sunset,
> In the loveliest of her vallies,
> We have spread our humble pallets,
> > On the green breast of the earth;
>
> And around our blazing campfire,
> Thoughtful faces glowed with feeling,
> While around our rude rock table,
> > Little faces shone with mirth.[61]

This narrative poem describes the beauties and the hazards of crossing the Appalachian Mountains. From her continuing narrative, we can follow the approximate route she followed, which corresponds closely to that of modern automobile routes: From Jamestown–Springfield–New Garden, North Carolina, to Hawk's Nest (modern Hawk's Nest State Park) and Beckley, West Virginia, and eventually following the course of the Kanahwa River to Point Pleasant on the Ohio River, with Gallipolis, Ohio, just across the river. To arrive in Gallipolis was to arrive in the land of the free.

The indomitable Delphina had faced a particularly painful challenge after her husband's death: James Ruffin Mendenhall, Eliza's son and Delphina's stepson, did not share his stepmother's aversion to slavery. On one of her expeditions to free territory with some of her slaves, she was overtaken in Virginia by her stepson who was brandishing copies of a new law prohibiting the freeing of slaves by will. Such a law was passed by the 1860–1861 session of the North Carolina General Assembly. On the complaint of James Ruffin Mendenhall, the Virginia police turned the Quaker lady and her charges back again to North Carolina. But Delphina won in the end: The North Carolina Supreme Court validated the will of George C. Mendenhall in November, 1864, setting the slaves free.

Delphina shared the profound anxieties and troubles that the Civil War brought to the civilian population of the South, but she was not to be intimidated. In 1863, she wrote to her friend John B. Crenshaw in Richmond concerning a black woman named Harriet Lane, then living in Petersburg, Virginia. She asked Crenshaw to get her papers for Harriet to go to Baltimore, in Union territory, with a white family, under a flag of truce. The white man was to be provided with a power of attorney to set Harriet free in Baltimore. The ever-helpful and influential Crenshaw provided the papers, and Harriet Lane eventually arrived safely in Baltimore with her protectors. Delphina's emotional involvement with Harriet Lane comes out in her correspondence with Crenshaw. At a time when Petersburg was under siege by the Union Army, she told him of her deep gratitude for his help for Harriet Lane. "If she were still in Petersburg," she wrote, "I sometimes think I should have to go to the asylum."[62]

Harriet Lane follows flag of truce to Baltimore.

We learn of another African–American woman who was the object of much concern to Delphina. Her name was Amy Alston, and in some way she had been left behind in North Carolina when her husband was emancipated and sent to Ohio before the war. In 1863, the husband sent $1,000 to Delphina to purchase his wife. Delphina complied and then appealed to John B. Crenshaw to provide Amy Alston with a "passport" to join her husband in Ohio. Her plan was to consign her to Miles White, a veteran of the removal effort thirty years earlier, who was then living in Ohio.

In yet another case, Delphina traveled to the enemy (i.e., Union) lines in Virginia on a humanitarian mission. It was in November of 1864. In a letter to Judith Crenshaw, wife of John B., she told of how she had started fourteen of her freed slaves on their way to freedom. One J. Harris was with her when she left by train from Greensboro with her charges, at two o'clock in the morning. Improbable as it seems, she claimed that it was all quite legal because she had passports for her charges to cross enemy lines and go on to Baltimore, and from there to Ohio. When the train arrived at Murphy's Station the next day, they found the depot burned down, but they were able to find shelter from the rain in the home of a Friend, Joshua Pretlow. But we will let her tell her own story:

> We went from there across Blackwater to Lawrence's — then to Henry Hare's then to William H. Hare's — then to Suffolk — then to the Yankee picket post — 22nd could not go to Norfolk without permission of General Shelby — which would require 3 to 5 days — After only one hour of deliberation, we felt satisfied to send the immigrants on — to Norfolk. A boat was going out next day to Baltimore — and I hope they are now safe in Ohio.[63]

When Delphina and her companion returned to Jamestown, they had colds from exposure but were otherwise well pleased with their mission. Surprising as this appears to us in the midst of a cruel war, it also caused astonishment to the people along the way. How was it possible to get the "passports"? Delphina explained that she got statements from respected local citizens as to the need for her charges to leave, got a certificate and seal from the clerk of court, and sent the package to Richmond, where it was deemed sufficient for issuing the "passports." We may be sure that her good friend, John B. Crenshaw, had a hand in it also.

The fourteen persons taken to the Yankee Picket Post in Virginia arrived safely in Ohio. By November, 1865, Delphina wrote to John B. Crenshaw that only seven remained of those left to her by the will of George C. Mendenhall. These seven were exempt from the draft, because they were working on the railroad.

There were other problems for Delphina on the Mendenhall estates in wartime North Carolina. Food and other provisions were so scarce that the departure for freedom for some left very welcome provisions for others. The joy of humanitarian service was mingled with the heavy burden of sustaining a small colony of people with very scarce resources.

When the war finally ended and the national will had vindicated the long struggle of Friends against slavery, Delphina Mendenhall could not refrain from bursting out in poetry. She celebrated universal emancipation with "The Freedmen's Song":

> The Freedmen's Song
> Midst glorious Alleluiahs, loud
>   Resounding through the holy heavens,
> Our Father's tender ear still bowed
>   To deep, low groans — our chain is riven!

Four long, sad, and dreary years,
   We heard the raging Red Sea roar,
The awful Sea of Blood and Tears —
   Its surges stilled, we tread the shore.

Free! Free as the mountain breezes are —
   Free as the deep's blue bounding wave —
Free as the beaming of the star —
   Free from the cradle to the grave!

Four millions disenthralled we stand —
   Four millions with unfettered feet —
Four millions with unshackled hand —
   To raise toward the Mercy–Seat.[64]

XIII

After The War

These impoverished war refugees [the North Carolina Quakers] passed through Baltimore, where their rough, homespun clothing and bundles with their meager possessions in them, made a sorry sight.

By the end of the war, the remnant of the Society of Friends in North Carolina was a beleaguered and reduced family. By some estimates, not more than 2,000 remained, and they were in poor circumstances. Virtually all of them had relatives in the West, and many of those who remained had been prevented from going there by the war. Now, they were free to go and the prospects were very attractive, for the South, by contrast, had been devastated. Quakers had suffered because their young men had often fled or been conscripted — which often meant prison. Many of the farms had been left to the care of women who had children to care for, and who had little skill in farming in any case. Both Confederate and Union armies had carried off horses and cattle, as well as stores of grain. The relative prosperity of the West was a powerful magnet.

The Civil War was a tragedy for all North Carolinians, but it affected Quakers in a special way. It was the *coup de grace* after years of tension and troubles arising from their opposition to slavery. For three generations they had been under the burden of living in a slaveholding society, while their consciences had been progressively tendered on the injustice of slavery. For two generations they had struggled to free themselves of the taint of owning slaves and to bring an end to the slavery that surrounded them. As the Quaker

After The War

planters had freed their slaves, they found themselves at a disadvantage competing with slave labor.

When the Ordinance of 1787 declared that the Northwest Territory (later to be divided into the states of Ohio, Indiana Illinois, Michigan, Wisconsin, and part of Minnesota) would

Map of Northwest Territory and future states.

remain forever free of slavery, Quakers were immediately interested in settling there. They did so in such great numbers that between 1800 and 1861, eighty–three meetings were laid down. The scattered meetings in South Carolina and Georgia belonging to North Carolina Yearly Meeting were among the earliest to disappear. In Pasquotank County, North Carolina, the ancient Symons Creek Meeting, founded in 1700, was laid down. Trent River Meeting picked up and moved as a body in 1800. It kept its officers and settled first in Pennsylvania and then in Ohio. New Garden Meeting, seat of the yearly meeting since 1813, gave out 245 certificates of removal representing one hundred families and eighty–three individuals between 1801 and 1866.

Much has been written about the changed nature of the Southern economy during that period, especially following the introduction of the cotton gin during the 1790s, and always there are many motives for large movements of populations. Writing at the end of the nineteenth century, Stephen B. Weeks emphasized the ethnic factor, pointing out that the Carolina Quakers were "Teutons," responding to a primal urge to keep moving like their remote European ancestors. Today, we might discount that motivation. Economics and technology certainly had a lot to do with this migration, but the transcendent reason was probably slavery.

The experience of Zachariah Dicks and South Carolina Friends illustrates the point dramatically. There was a widespread conviction, common among non–Quakers as well as Quakers, that the troubles in the South were the result of the curse of slavery. A righteous God was punishing the people for their sins. Confirming this view in the early 1800s was the agony of Haiti, where a ruling elite was deposed, and many massacred, during a terrifying slave revolt. Panic spread among slaveholders everywhere.

Into this charged atmosphere came Zachariah Dicks from Cane Creek Meeting in North Carolina. A respected Friend who had traveled widely in the ministry, he was believed to possess the gift of prophecy. Alarming, indeed, was his warning to Friends in South Carolina, between 1800 and 1804, that they must "come out of slavery." "He told them that if they did not their fate would be that of the slaughtered islanders. This produced a sort of panic and removals to Ohio commenced."[65]

The movement of Friends to the West after the Civil War is thus to be seen as an acceleration of a process that had long been underway. Times had changed since the many years of struggling over the mountains with wagons pulled by oxen or horses. The railroad age had arrived, so that while some, especially the young men, went over the mountains, the overwhelming preference now was the long, circuitous route by way of Baltimore prefigured by the famous odyssey of Delphina's slaves. The stream of emigrants was encouraged by an earlier emigrant named Addison Coffin. A son of Vestal Coffin, and cousin of Levi Coffin, he worked with Levi in the defense of slaves seeking freedom and in the Underground Railroad. He was also, by nature, an adventurer and pioneer. Long before the Civil War he had settled in Indiana where he remained active in antislavery work and was among those who formed the Anti–Slavery Yearly Meeting of Friends in that state. With the end of the war, he felt it his duty to help his fellow North Carolinians emigrate from the South. Becoming, in effect, a travel agent, he arranged for thousands to make this journey by train from Greensboro, North Carolina, to Richmond, Indiana. He claimed to have arranged transport for 14,000 people, one–tenth of whom were Quakers.[66]

These impoverished war refugees passed through Baltimore, where their rough, homespun clothing and meager bundles with all their possessions in them made a sorry sight. Friends in Baltimore helped them as they were able. One of those who came under the burden of this stream of impoverished humanity was Francis T.

King, a well-to-do Quaker who was involved in important matters in Baltimore, and had already acted in behalf of North Carolina Friends. He had traveled there on religious and humanitarian service during the war, carrying a pass signed by Abraham Lincoln. This pass is now in the Friends Historical Collection at Guilford College. Francis King had a good understanding of the problems of North Carolina.

With other Friends, Francis T. King formed the Baltimore Association to give aid to Quakers in North Carolina who had suffered in the war. He made thirty-five trips to that state, encouraging Friends to remain and rebuild their lives and their institutions. He also traveled to Friends meetings throughout the United States, England, and Ireland raising money for this great effort to revitalize the life of the Society of Friends in North Carolina.

This was not a mere relief program. His view was that rebuilding — and in some cases creating — a school system was of prime importance. The Association helped organize and staff forty-one schools and, during the peak year of 1870, enrolled 2,774 pupils. Between 1865 and 1887 the Baltimore Association spent $138,300 on aid to North Carolina Friends. This included, in addition to schools, a model farm at Springfield (near High Point), crucial help to New Garden Boarding School, repairs to old meeting houses, and construction of new ones.

In the beginning, there was direct food relief, as well as clothing, for destitute Friends, especially in the Goldsboro area. But King was a great believer in self-reliance. He helped people to help themselves, and, in educational as well as agricultural work, he provided seed money but always required local persons to do their part in rebuilding their lives and institutions.

Work with freed slaves was a part of this program but took second place to the rebuilding of Quakerism in North Carolina.

There were six schools for freedmen in 1867 and twenty-one Sunday Schools with an estimated attendance of between 1,600 and 2,000. Nevertheless, by 1872, little more is heard from these schools in the Friends records. The important exception was the little school in Asheboro under the joint sponsorship of the New York Yearly Meeting of Friends and the Freedmen's Bureau. It was established in 1885. Six years later, in 1891, the decision was made to move the school to High Point, where it was to join a school that had been operated for black children since before the war by Quaker Solomon Isaac Blair. Before the Civil War, this school was illegal under North Carolina law, but Solomon Blair's Quaker concern was not to be diverted by a technicality.[67]

When the Asheboro school came to High Point, it went into a simple two-room building that had been built by Solomon Blair in 1867 when it finally became legal to operate schools for freed slaves. It also served as a church building for the newly freed slaves. This was the beginning of a major educational project in High Point, and at the heart of it was Solomon Isaac Blair. His grandson, the late publisher John Fries Blair of Winston-Salem, described him as

Solomon Blair's school for Negroes in High Point.

"one of God's noblemen," and the founding of the school as "an act of religious conviction and civic leadership." When the school was established, it served adults as well as children in order to address the needs of the freedmen who at the time were mostly illiterate and in need of every kind of training to meet the demands of freedom.[68]

As the school became established in High Point, it took the name of the High Point Normal and Industrial Institute. Sixty or seventy elementary children were crowded into each of the 20-foot by 20-foot rooms. Three years later, in 1894, the New York Yearly Meeting, observing the overcrowding and obvious need, purchased more land and undertook construction of a new and larger building. In this project, both white and black citizens of High Point raised money, which, when joined with the funds from New York, came to $2,900. In this new building, the school grew to an enrollment of 287 students with a faculty of nine. Male students raised food on the adjoining farm, and girls used their training in food preparation to supply the dining room.

James's Plantation School, North Carolina.
Reprinted with permission of the
North Carolina Division of Archives and History.

By 1900 it was necessary to expand again. The 1894 building had been a frame building, but for the new one in 1900, students used their skills in brick-making, masonry and carpentry to erect a fine three-story brick structure. Even the furniture was made by students with skills learned at the school. The girls were taught sewing, cooking, basket-weaving, and dressmaking. The fine 1900 building was erected with generous help from Ellen L. Congdon, a New York Quaker. These skilled students now began to serve the larger community, as High Point citizens called on them for doing repairs. It is reported that they also built an eight-room house. The students operated a shoe repair shop and a blacksmith shop.

The original Institute building was destroyed by fire in 1910, at which time six new buildings were constructed to create a campus for the flourishing school. Included was a barn for the farm animals.

By 1923, the school had grown so phenomenally that New York Yearly Meeting could no longer bear the expense of operating it. Consequently, it decided to sell the property to the City of High

Teaching the Freedmen.
Reprinted with permission of the
North Carolina Division of Archives and History

Point, which used it for an accredited high school for black children.

Thus ended the fifty–six year life of the Quaker project undertaken in the wake of the Civil War to help freedmen make the transition from slavery to freedom. The courage, patience, and dedication of Solomon Isaac Blair had been vindicated, and the generous help of the New York Yearly Meeting of Friends, in cooperation with many other good and generous people, had borne fruit.

The coming of school integration in the 1960s indicated the fulfillment of the promise made to the black community by the Civil War. Sometime during the 1920s, the new public school had been renamed the William Penn High School, as they said, "in honor of the famous Quaker founder of Pennsylvania and in honor of those Quakers who played such a vital role in the history of the school." It was appropriate that as the William Penn High School was merged into the new integrated T. Wingate Andrews High School in 1968, the first principal should be S. E. Burford, the last principal of William Penn. Burford had been the principal of William Penn since 1933, and had gained the respect of both black and white communities. An alumnus writes that he "always insisted that William Penn only provided us with an opportunity for achievement that had to be matched by our own scholarship, sacrifice and faith in ourselves."

As this is written, a group of black and white citizens of High Point, operating under the name of the William Penn Foundation, Inc., is engaged in a long–range campaign to renovate and preserve the campus of William Penn High School as a historic site and community center. The school has been listed on the National Register of Historic Places. Included in the William Penn Foundation's assessment of the role of the High Point Normal and Industrial Institute is the assertion that the training in furniture making helped prepare a base of skilled workers for the burgeoning furniture industry of High Point.[68]

William Penn Auditorium, a national historic place.

Although it was not a Quaker institution, the Slater Industrial Academy for Negroes at Winston–Salem, North Carolina, involved a number of Quakers. It was established in 1892 by Dr. Simon Green Atkins, a slave–born native of Chatham County, North Carolina. Two northern Quaker women, "Mrs. Payson and Mrs. Woolson" joined Mrs. Atkins on the first faculty of the school. William A. Blair, a son of Solomon Isaac Blair who founded the High Point Normal and Industrial Institute, was at that time a banker and attorney in Winston–Salem. He served on the board of directors of Slater Academy and helped in other ways. John J. Blair, another son of Solomon, was at the time superintendent of the Winston–Salem public schools. A third son of Solomon, David, had studied under John W. Woody at New Garden Boarding School and had come to admire him. The three brothers persuaded Woody to come from Friends University in Wichita, Kansas, to help launch Slater Academy.

John W. Woody stayed at Slater Academy for nine years and served in many capacities. He was business agent, fund-raiser, promoter, and teacher and was known to the students as the "white president" of Slater Academy. Mary Chawner Woody, his wife, was not one to sit idly by. An activist and concerned Friend wherever she went, she threw herself into the cause of Slater Academy as a promoter and fundraiser. She especially solicited the assistance of Quakers in Philadelphia and New York. Slater was a school for blacks and obviously filled a need at the time. In 1925 it became Winston–Salem Teachers College, and in 1969 the state legislature transformed it into Winston-Salem State University.

At all times, both of the Woodys made it clear that they believed persons of all races were equal in the sight of God. Living in the shadow of the Civil War and in a period when reactionary forces were determined to prevent equal opportunity for African–Americans, they were aggressive advocates of civil rights for all.[70]

XIV

Unfinished Business

Separate but equal became the new norm in education, and Quakers in North Carolina generally embraced it.

Fernando Cartland, in *Southern Heroes*, brings us an excerpt from the minutes of Hopewell Friends Meeting, near Winchester, Virginia, at the end of the Civil War. Hopewell had been an important sojourning point for Friends from Pennsylvania who eventually settled in North Carolina, and this selection reflects the initial reaction of Friends in North Carolina as well. It reads:

> We hail the return of peace and the establishment of law and order throughout the land, bringing with it the abolition of slavery and the ultimate enfranchisement of the negro race, a consumation for which our society has long and faithfully labored.[71]

Mary Mendenhall Hobbs, granddaughter of Richard Mendenhall, and grandniece of George C. Mendenhall, reminisced in a letter to Allen Jay:

> We had been a little band of believers in peace in the midst of war, of antislavery abolitionists in the heart of slave territory, of hearts almost to a unit loyal to the Union in the midst of secession. The way had not been strewn with flowers. Espionage and a degree of persecution had drawn us closer

together and intensified both our principles and our prejudices. We had had almost no intercourse with the outside world....[72]

This feeling of isolation and loneliness tempered the joy felt by Friends at the end of slavery. A hundred years of working against slavery, freeing slaves, and defending those who were free, added to the hardships of the war and nearly exhausted the energies of North Carolina Friends. Besides, they felt that their obligation to the blacks had been met in the Proclamation of Emancipation. Furthermore, Friends felt so overwhelmed by their own problems that, in their reduced numbers and in their poverty, there was not much left to help others. As for leadership, the bulk of the ardent reformers had long since departed for free territory in Indiana, Ohio, and other points west. It might be argued that those who remained were of a more compromising bent than those who left. Yet, for whatever reason, the long special relationship between North Carolina Quakers and African–Americans entered a new phase in the decades following the Civil War. There was — and is — a lingering feeling of mutual confidence between them. Nevertheless, as race relations evolved in American society, the line of separation that remained in the South permeated the Quaker community as well.

Separate but equal became the new norm in education, and Quakers embraced it. Even the laudable High Point Normal and Industrial Institute was unconsciously, but effectively, segregated. As New Garden Boarding School was transformed into Guilford College in 1888, with a powerful assist from Francis T. King, it did not take the bold step of recruiting black students, as did, for example, Berea College in Kentucky, and Oberlin in Ohio. In that period, more attention was paid to developing separate institutions for blacks. In Greensboro, Quaker D. W. B. Benbow was instrumental in founding the North Carolina Agricultural and Technical

College, and another Quaker, Robert Frazier, long served as chairman of its board of trustees in the mid-twentieth century. In separate but equal, the Quaker emphasis was on the equal, but, in general, separate was assumed. Guilford College, under tacit instructions from the board of trustees, did not admit black students until 1962, eight years after the Supreme Court decision requiring integration of public universities. On the other hand, the administration and faculty were ready for integration some time before the trustees.

Inasmuch as Quakers are a national and international society, there was always encouragement from the larger Quaker community to be more aggressive in promoting racial justice. One important early venture in the post-war period was undertaken by a Philadelphia Quaker named Yardley Warner. His interest in the freedmen took the form of a housing development in south Greensboro, in conjunction with the Freedmen's Bureau. There, he built a model village for the former slaves. It consisted of modest frame houses with space around each one for a small lawn and garden. There was also provision for small businesses to be run by the blacks themselves. It proved to be very popular and had to be expanded several times beyond the original plan. For many years it provided low-cost housing for black families in Greensboro, and was known as Warnersville. The writer remembers it as it survived in 1948, by then much deteriorated and becoming a slum. However, it retained some of the form of the original village. In 1965, it was demolished to make way for the urban renewal project known as Hampton Homes, honoring a black physician who was a civic leader and the first black member of the Greensboro City Council. This attractive development off South Elm-Eugene Street continues to provide low-cost housing for many Greensboro families in the spirit of Yardley Warner's purpose.

Warner is rightly honored as a person of exceptional dedication to his chosen cause, in the tradition of John Woolman. A native of Bucks County, Pennsylvania, he was reared in a home which was a station on the Underground Railroad. He is credited with having established some thirty schools for the Friends Freedmen's Association in North Carolina and Tennessee. He rejected the notion of black inferiority, which was assumed even by many friends of the blacks. Instead, he attributed any lack of ambition and trustworthiness in the freed slave to "200 years of teaching how to do nothing — i.e., how to get along with doing as little as possible."[73]

Because Warner was from the North, lived among the ex-slaves and worked with them, he was scorned by many whites as a "carpetbagger." He suffered taunting and a measure of persecution for his dedication to the African-American community. In the last years of his life, he lived in the Springfield community with his second wife. This man, who had given his entire life to causes that Friends applaud, found himself walking to Friends meeting in his declining years, looking "tired and bedraggled. The other Friends always had carriages, but not the Warners." Nell Craig observed in the *Greensboro Daily News* that, "even the Friends were not always as thoughtful as they might have been of these people whose work with ex-slaves made them outcasts by other white people."[74]

A bronze plaque now marks the location of the original Warnersville. It says:

> Yardley Warner, 1815–1885, lawyer, teacher, preacher. Born in Bucks County, Pennsylvania, known as the "freedmans friend" for his unselfish and untiring work in behalf of freed slaves. He sold one-half acre lots to freed men and established a school for Negroes in this area in 1867. He was a Quaker by faith and a minister to all mankind. Warnersville was named after this great humanitar-

ian. He died in Bush Hill, N. C., and was buried in the Cemetary of Springfield Monthly Meeting of Friends near High Point, N. C.
Presented by Conrad L. Raiford,
Born in Warnersville: 1907

Plaque honoring Yardley Warner in Greensboro.
Photo reprinted with permission of the Greensboro Historical Museum.

Another effort in behalf of racial justice in North Carolina during the first century after the Civil War was that of the American Friends Service Committee. The national offices of this body are in Philadelphia, and a regional office was opened in North Carolina in 1949. For many years the office was located in Greensboro, was later moved to High Point, then was transferred to Atlanta, Georgia. Early work of the AFSC in the post World War II period was in the field of international relations, but as the civil rights movement got underway, much of the work was in that area. The committee carried on an active program among businessmen and industrialists to provide equal opportunity for minorities and women. It became especially active in conducting workshops and providing expert counsel to administrators and teachers in preparation for integration of the schools. Since there was vigorous opposition to the whole integration movement by a large part of the white population in the South, this program became highly controversial. North Carolina Friends were active in local committees of the Service Committee, and there was support by many members of Friends meetings, although at the same time there was a degree of opposition.[75]

As racial integration of the public schools finally became a reality by court order, it became a real challenge to many Quaker administrators and teachers in the public school system. In positions of special responsibility, we may cite Sarah Mendenhall Brown, who was vice-chair of the board of education in Greensboro; Nathaniel Shope, superintendent of Wayne County schools; Clifford Winslow, chair of the board of education of Perquimans County; Shelby Shore, who served on the board of directors of Yadkin County schools and on the board of directors of the North Carolina School Boards Association. Governor Hunt appointed her as chair of the North Carolina Youth Advisory Council in 1979. This is only a representative list, not an exhaustive one. Many Quakers have helped to smooth the way for minorities in the state.

In 1955, some members of New Garden Meeting brought a concern to the monthly meeting regarding the integration of the local (Guilford) public school. They were liberated by the monthly meeting to proceed by taking their concern to the local school board. The letter the group presented to the board applauded the Supreme Court decision of 1954 mandating school integration and pledged the signers to support a decision of the board to carry out the order in the school where their own children were attending. Thirty-four persons, including a few non-Friends, signed the letter. Feelings were running high in the community when the *Greensboro Daily News* chose to print the Quaker letter on its front page. The reaction was immediate. Signers received abusive and threatening phone calls. The person who suffered the most owned a flourishing business in the village and found his old friends and customers turning against him. So many cancelled their accounts that he was forced out of business and had to leave the state. The news of this incident spread quickly all over the world, and support for the signers came from churches and individuals in other parts of the country.

Even so, in the long run integration of the public schools in North Carolina proceeded more smoothly than in many other places. In Greensboro, Ben L. Smith, the progressive superintendent of public schools, gave credit for the peaceful transition to "the liberal views of the Friends Society of which there are many members," and "the Jewish element that numbers many of Greensboro's leading businessmen and civic-minded citizens."[76]

The churches, however, including even Friends meetings, remained segregated. Observing this phenomenon, black activists began trying to break the church barrier. On rare occasions, someone would bring a black friend to a Quaker meeting. At least once when this occurred at New Garden Meeting, some Friends rose and left the room. At First Friends Meeting in Greensboro, in 1952, ushers refused to seat several African-American visitors at a morning service for worship. When this became known, there was objection from the membership, and much soul searching followed. A survey of members showed that a large majority would not have objected to having the visitors seated. The monthly meeting proceeded to adopt a policy permitting people of all races to be seated without distinction.

In the following years, African–Americans began to be welcomed to Friends meetings, but few came. As blacks acquired a new ethnic pride, there began to be pressure on them to avoid fraternizing with whites, so as not to appear to be subservient "Uncle Toms." In at least one instance, a black person was ready to join New Garden Meeting, when some of her black friends persuaded her not to. Later, however, there were scattered instances of black persons joining Friends at New Garden and other meetings. Very gradually the walls of separation have eroded, though freedom of choice has not resulted in a flood of black persons joining Friends meetings.

As for Guilford College, there have been some black students since the breakthrough of 1962, associated in part with the World Gathering of Friends at Guilford in 1967. Under the administration of President Grimsley Hobbs, there was active recruitment of black students, which has continued since that time. There are also a number of black members of the faculty and staff. New Garden Friends School, which is presently located on a corner of the Guilford College campus, has emphasized racial and ethnic diversity since its founding in 1972.

Ironically, the Quaker insistence on racial equality for more than 300 years has succeeded beyond all expectations, often overtaking the Quakers themselves. Today, American society as a whole has embraced the doctrine, and secular forces are among its strongest supporters. To remain racially intolerant has become a handicap for those looking for employment in the private, as well as in the public sectors. One of the great world–wide campaigns of our time has been that against the apartheid system of South Africa. Though many Quakers support this campaign actively, and students at Quaker colleges have been among its most enthusiastic supporters, the cause crosses all lines of society. The world has taken to out–Quakering the Quakers.

From Thomas Newby's awakening to our own time is a span of well over 200 years. In a way that Friends could not foresee — and even deplored — slavery came to an end. Their faithfulness was fulfilled by the Emancipation Proclamation. The awakening of the descendants of the slaves a century after the Civil War brought about the Civil Rights Act of 1964, paving the way for the fulfillment of the Quaker dream.

But history never stands still. Recent stirrings indicate dissatisfaction with the *status quo*— which is as it should be. There are new dimensions to a proper relationship among all members of society which are just now appearing over the horizon. A new generation is called to mold them to the needs of the twenty-first century.

Endnotes

¹North Carolina Yearly Meeting Minutes, 1704–1804; 1813–1991, Belvidere File, Friends Historical Collection, Guilford College, Greensboro, NC.

²Stephen B. Weeks, *Southern Quakers and Slavery* (Baltimore: Johns Hopkins University Press, 1896), 141, 142.

³Galatians 3:28.

⁴William Blassingame, *The Slave Community; Plantation Life in the Antebellum South* (New York: Oxford University Press, 1972), 164, citing Fletcher Green, *Ferry Hill Plantation Journal,* January 4, 1838 (Chapel Hill: University of North Carolina, 1961).

⁵Harvey Wish, *Slavery in the South* (New York: Farrar, Straus, 1964), 198.

⁶Wish, 28, 29.

⁷Blassingame, chapter 5.

⁸Ibid., 96.

⁹Ibid., 167–169.

¹⁰Ibid., 170.

¹¹Joshua Evans, *Journal of the Lives, Religious Exercises and Labours in the work of the Ministry of Joshua Evans and John Hunt,* in *Friends Miscellany,* Vol. 10, edited by John and Isaac Comly (Philadelphia: Byberry; printed by J. Richards, 1837), 173–174. Also, Weeks, 110.

¹²Phillips P. Moulton, ed., *The Journal and Major Essays of John Woolman* (Richmond, IN: Friends United Press, 1989), 69.

¹³Blassingame, 196.

¹⁴Ibid., 7, 8.

¹⁵Ibid., 210–21.

[16] Ibid., 85, 86.

[17] George P. Rawick, ed., *The American Slave: A Composite Autobiography*. Vol. II (Westport, CT: Greenwood Publishing Co. 1972), 55.

[18] Levi Coffin, *Reminiscences of Levi Coffin*, 2nd ed. (Cincinnati: R. Clarke and Co., 1880), 15.

[19] Herbert Aptheker, *American Negro Slave Revolts* (New York: Columbia University Press, 1973), 289.

[20] Thomas E. Drake, *Quakers and Slavery in America* (New Haven: Yale University Press, 1950), 10.

[21] Weeks, 67.

[22] Ibid., 68.

[23] Henry G. Hood, Jr., *The Public Career of John Archdale (1642–1717)* (Greensboro, NC: North Carolina Friends Historical Society, 1976).

[24] Weeks, 262.

[25] New Garden Monthly Meeting Minutes, 10-28-1767, Friends Historical Collection, Guilford College, Greensboro, NC.

[26] Ibid. 8-29-1768.

[27] Slave Papers, Perquimans County Court, 1759–1799, North Carolina State Archives, Raleigh, NC.

[28] Hiram H. Hilty, *Toward Freedom for All* (Richmond, IN: Friends United Press, 1984), 34. Correspondence of the Meeting for Sufferings, Item A–1, Friends Historical Collection, Guilford College, Greensboro, NC.

[29] William S. Gaston to the standing committee, December 3, 1809, Correspondence of the Meeting for Sufferings, Friends Historical Collection, Guilford College, Greensboro, NC.

[30] Hilty, 56.

[31] *The Life, Travels and Opinions of Benjamin Lundy*, by his children (Philadelphia: W. D. Parrish, 1847) 22, 23, 206.

[32] Hilty, 41–43.

33Ibid., 66, 67.

34Thomas P. Devereaux, ed., *North Carolina Reports 12, Cases In Law argued before the Supreme Court of North Carolina, December Term, 1826, to June Term, 1828* (Raleigh, NC: 1916),120–123.

35Hilty, 64. Meeting for Sufferings, Items 41, 44, Friends Historical Collection, Guilford College, Greensboro, NC.

36Hilty, 68. *Acts passed by the General Assembly of N.C., 1812–1831* (Raleigh, NC: 1832). Algie I. Newlin with collaboration of Harvey Newlin, *The Newlin Family, Ancestors and Descendants of John and Mary Pyle Newlin* (Greensboro, NC: Published by author, 1965), n.p.

37Hilty, passim. Meeting for Sufferings, 1–31–1851, Friends Historical Collection, Guilford College, Greensboro, NC.

38James Iredell, ed., *North Carolina Reports 34, Cases In Law Argued Before the Supreme Court of North Carolina, June Term, 1851* (Raleigh, NC: 1917), 41.

39Slave Papers, Perquimans County Court, 1759–1799. Hilty, 70.

40Meeting for Sufferings, *A Narrative of Some of the Proceedings of North Carolina Yearly Meeting on the Subject of Slavery Within Its Limits* (Greensboro, NC: Swain and Sherwood, 1848), 66.

41Epistle of Advice, North Carolina Yearly Meeting, November 7, 1843, Friends Historical Collection, Guilford College, Greensboro, NC.

42Hilty, 90, citing Purifoy, *Journal of Southern History,* 32, August 1966, 327–328.

43Meeting for Sufferings, items 184, 187, 188 for Julius Pringle affair, Friends Historical Collection, Guilford College, Greensboro, NC. Also, *The Friend*, 6, No. 9 (December 1, 1832), 65–66.

44Nicholas Halasz, *The Rattling Chains* (New York: D. McKay Co., 1966), 115.

45Record of Wills, D File 01111, Guilford County, NC 1850. Hilty, 104.

46Meeting for Sufferings, Item 107, Friends Historical Collection, Guilford College, Greensboro, NC. Hilty, 76.

[47] Meeting for Sufferings, Minute Books 25 and 41, Friends Historical Collection, Guilford College, Greensboro, NC. Hilty, 77.

[48] U.B. Phillips, *American Negro Slavery*, (New York: D. Appleton and Co., 1918), 413–414.

[49] Moulton, 50, 198–237.

[50] This and other material on Levi Coffin, from Coffin, *Reminiscences of Levi Coffin,* 2nd ed. (Cincinnati: R. Clarke and Co., 1880).

[51] Papers of Julia W. Outland (nee Julia W. Copeland), Friends Historical Collection, Guilford College, Greensboro, NC.

[52] Isham Cox, Letters from a Slaveholder, Drawer 13, Friends Historical Collection, Guilford College, Greensboro, NC. Hilty, 98.

[53] North Carolina Yearly Meeting minutes, November 5, 1861, Friends Historical Collection, Guilford College, Greensboro, NC.

[54] Fernando T. Cartland, *Southern Heroes* (Cambridge, MA: Riverside Press, 1895), 288.

[55] Seth B. Hinshaw, *The Carolina Quaker Experience*, (Greensboro, NC: North Carolina Friends Historical Society, 1984), 151, citing Hugh T. Lefler and Albert R. Newsome, *North Carolina, The History of a Southern State* (Chapel Hill: University of North Carolina Press, rev. ed. 1963), 396.

[56] Patrick Sowle, "The Quaker Conscript in Confederate North Carolina," *Quaker History*, vol. 46, no. 2 (Autumn 1967), 99,100.

[57] Mary Daniels Johnstone, coordinator, *The Heritage of Wayne County, North Carolina* (Winston–Salem, NC: The Wayne County Historical Associaton and the Society in cooperation with Hunter Publishing Co., c. 1982).

[58] Courtesy of Ruth P. Harper.

[59] Sally W. Stockard, *The History of Guilford County, North Carolina* (Greensboro, NC: The Guilford County Genealogical Society, republication, 1983).

[60] Record of Wills, D File 1111, 45–53, Guilford County, NC, recorded 8th day, second month, 1859, probated May Term 1860.

[61] Delphina E. Mendenhall's poetry, Box 20, Friends Historical Collection, Guilford College, Greensboro, NC.

[62] W. H. S. Wood Papers, 7-25-1864, Friends Historical Collection, Guilford College, Greensboro, NC.

[63] Ibid., 8-1-1864.

[64] Mendenhall poetry.

[65] Weeks, 267, citing O'Neall.

[66] Addison Coffin, "Early Settlements of Friends in North Carolina, Traditions and Reminiscences," typed copy in Friends Historical Collection, Guilford College, Greensboro, NC.

[67] Weeks, 310-316.

[68] *The Best Kept Secret* (brochure), William Penn Foundation, High Point, NC, 1984.

[69] High Point Normal and Industrial Institute File, Friends Historical Collection, Guilford College, Greensboro, NC.

[70] Mary Edith Hinshaw, *Pioneers in Quaker Education* (Greensboro, NC: North Carolina Friends Historical Society and Publications Board of North Carolina Yearly Meeting of Friends, 1992), 50-57.

[71] Cartland, 364.

[72] Allen Jay, *Autobiography of Allen Jay, born 1831, died 1910* (Philadelphia: The John C. Winston Co., 1910), 168-169.

[73] James Woodhams Hood, "The Indefatigable Yardley Warner" (High Point, NC: Presentation at Springfield Memorial Association Meeting, August 9, 1990). Stafford A. Warner, *Yardley Warner: The Freedman's Friend.* (Didcot: The Wessex Press, 1957).

[74] Nell Craig, *Greensboro Daily News*, 1 June, 1941.

[75] William Bagwell, *School Desegregation in the Carolinas* (Columbia, SC: University of South Carolina Press, 1972), 112-115.

[76] Ibid., 191-207.

BIBLIOGRAPHICAL

This book is based primarily on the author's *Toward Freedom for All*, published by the Friends United Press in 1984. References to "Hilty" in this text refer to that book. Much of the material in both books is drawn from "North Carolina Quakers and Slavery," the author's dissertation for the Ph.D. degree at Duke University in 1968.

Below is a list of works cited in this book:

Acts passed by the General Assembly of North Carolina, 1812–1831. Raleigh, NC.

Aptheker, Herbert. *American Negro Slave Revolts*. New York: Columbia University Press, 1943.

Arnett, Ethel. *William Swaim, Fighting Editor*. Greensboro, NC: Piedmont Press, 1963.

Bagwell, William. *School Desegregation in the Carolinas*. Columbia, SC: University of South Carolina Press, 1972.

The Best Kept Secret (brochure). High Point, NC: The William Penn Foundation, 1984.

Blassingame, William. *The Slave Community; Plantation Life in the Antebellum South*. New York: Oxford University Press, 1972.

Cartland, Fernando T. *Southern Heroes*. Cambridge, Mass: Riverside Press, 1895.

Coffin, Levi. *Reminiscences of Levi Coffin*. Cincinnati: R. Clarke and Co., 1880.

Devereaux, Thomas P., ed. *North Carolina Reports 12, Cases at Law Argued and Determined in the Supreme Court of North Carolina, December Term, 1826 to June Term 1828.* Raleigh, NC: 1916.

Drake, Thomas E. *Quakers and Slavery in America.* New Haven: Yale University Press, 1950.

Evans, Joshua. *Journal of the Lives, Religious Exercises and Labours in the Work of Ministry of Joshua Evans and John Hunt* in *Friends Miscellany, vol. 10.* Eds. John and Isaac Comly. Philadelphia: Byberry. Printed by J. Richards, 1837.

Friends Historical Collection. Greensboro, NC: Guilford College.

    Coffin, Addison. "Early Settlements of Friends in North Carolina, Traditions and Reminiscences" (typed copy).

    Cox, Isham. Letters from a Slaveholder, Drawer 13.

    High Point Normal and Industrial File.

    Meeting for Sufferings, Records of, North Carolina Yearly Meeting.

    Delphina E. Mendenhall's Poetry, Box 20.

    New Garden Monthly Meeting Minutes, 10-28-1767.

    North Carolina Yearly Meeting Minutes, 1704-1804; 1813-1991.

    Papers of Julia W. Outland (nee Julia W. Copeland).

    W. H. S. Wood Papers. Greensboro, NC: Friends Historical Collection, Guilford College, Nov. 28, 1864.

Guilford County Record of Wills, D File 01111. Guilford County, NC.

Halasz, Nicholas. *The Rattling Chains.* New York: D. McKay Co., 1966.

Hilty, Hiram H. "North Carolina Quakers and Slavery," a dissertation for the Ph.D. degree. Durham, NC: Department of History, Duke University, 1968.

Toward Freedom for All. Richmond, IN: Friends United Press, 1984.

Hinshaw, Mary Edith. *Pioneers in Quaker Education.* Greensboro, NC: North Carolina Friends Historical Society and Publications Board of North Carolina Yearly Meeting of Friends, 1992.

Hinshaw, Seth B. *The Carolina Quaker Experience.* Greensboro, NC: North Carolina Friends Historical Society, 1984.

Hood, Henry G., Jr. *The Public Career of John Archdale (1642–1717).* Greensboro, NC: North Carolina Friends Historical Society, 1976.

Hood, James Woodhams, "The Indefatigable Yardley Warner." High Point, NC: Presentation at Springfield Memorial Association Meeting, August 19, 1990.

Iredell, James, ed. *North Carolina Reports, 34, Cases in Law Argued Before the Supreme Court of North Carolina, June Term, 1851,* Raleigh, NC: 1917, 41.

Jay, Allen. *Autobiography of Allen Jay, born 1831, died 1910.* Philadelphia: The John C. Winston Co., 1910.

Johnston, Mary Daniels, coordinator. *The Heritage of Wayne County, North Carolina* (pamphlet). Winston–Salem, NC: The Wayne County Historical Association and the society in cooperation with Hunter Publishing Com., c. 1982.

Lundy's children. *The Life, Travels and Opinions of Benjamin Lunday.* Philadelphia: W. D. Parrish, 1847.

Moulton, Phillips P. *The Journal and Major Essays of John Woolman.* Richmond, IN: Friends United Press, 1989.

Newlin, Algie I., with the collaboration of Harvey Newlin. *The Newlin Family, Ancestors and Descendants of John and Mary Pyle Newlin.* Greensboro, NC: Published by author, 1965.

Phillips, U. B. *American Negro Slavery.* New York: D. Appleton and Co., 1918.

Rawick, George P., ed. *The American Slave: A Composite Autobiography, Vol. II.* Westport, CT: Greenwood Publishing Co., 1972.

Slave Papers. Perquimans County Court, 1759–1799. North Carolina State Archives, Raleigh, NC.

Sowle, Patrick, "The Quaker Conscript in Confederate North Carolina," *Quaker History.* Haverford, PA: Friends Historical Association, Autumn, 1967.

Stockard, Sally W. *The History of Guilford County North Carolina.* Greensboro, NC: The Guilford County Genealogical Society (republication), 1983.

Warner, Stafford Allen. *Yardley Warner: The Freedman's Friend.* Didcot: The Wessex Press, 1957.

Weeks, Stephen B. *Southern Quakers and Slavery.* Baltimore: Johns Hopkins University Press, 1896.

Wish, Harvey. *Slavery in the South.* New York: Farrar, Straus, 1964.

INDEX

A

Abels, William, captain of the *American*, 62
Abolitionist Movement, 55
Abolitionist literature banned in NC, 66
Above ground railroad: 67; routes, 68; map, 70
African Concerns, Indiana Yearly Meeting Committee on, 69
African slavery introduced to America, 11
African slaves, war prisoners, 11
Albertson, Benjamin, frees slaves, 3
Albertson, Chalkley, frees slaves, 3
Albertson, Elihue, frees slaves, 5
Albertson, William, frees slaves, 3
Alston, Amy, ex–slave aided by Delphina Mendenhall, 91
American, brig: takes Quaker Free Negroes to Liberia, 38; sails for Liberia, 62
American Colonization Society, 36–40; 60–65
American Friends Service Committee, 109
Anderson, John, frees slaves, 5
Anti–Slavery Society, 74
Anti–Slavery Yearly Meeting of Friends in Indiana, 97
Aptheker, Herbert, historian, 17
Archdale, John, Quaker governor, 21
Arrington, William, rounds up freed slaves, 6
Asheboro, NC: Freedmen's school, 99
Atkins, Dr. Simon Green, slave–born founder of Slater Academy, 103
Aux Cayes, Haiti, destination for Quaker Free Negroes, 34

B

Baltimore Association: aids Quakers, 98; organizes schools, 98
Barbados charges Fox with inciting slaves to revolt, 19
Barnes, Jack, runaway slave, 75
Beals, Thomas, anti–slavery advocate, New Garden, 22
Beard, John A., Manumission Society member, 53
Benbow, D. W. B., Quaker, instrumental in founding NCA&T College, 106
Benson, Benjamin, Quakers gain his freedom, 51

Berea College in Kentucky, 106
Bibliography, 119
Blair, David, son of Solomon, 103
Blair, John Fries, publisher, grandson of Solomon, 99
Blair, John J., son of Solomon Blair and superintendent of Winston–Salem public schools, 103
Blair, Solomon Isaac, founder of Quaker school, 99; 102
Blair, William A., son of Solomon Blair, trustee of Slater Academy, 103
Bond for each freed slave, slaveholders required to post, 26
Brown, John, antislavery activist guest in Quaker home, 79
Brown, Sarah Mendenhall, vice chair of Greensboro public schools board of education, 110
Buchanan, U. S. President, 86
Burford, S. E., principal of William Penn High School and T. Wingate Andrews High School, 102

C

Caldwell, Dr. David, educator, slaveholder, 77
Cane Creek Monthly Meeting, 4; 14; 22
Cane Creek Quaker community, 22
Carson, Dr. James Green, plantation owner, 12
Carter, John, pleads for military exemption for Quakers, 83
Cartland, Fernando, author of *Southern Heroes*, 77; 83; 84; 85; 105
Cedar Creek Monthly Meeting, VA, 23
Centre Monthly Meeting, 41
Chickahominy tribe, 20
Civil Rights Act of 1964, 54
Civil War: 81; aftermath of, 94
Cofer, "Aunt" Betty, on slave life, 13
Coffin, Addison: aids runaway slaves, 72; antislavery activist and Indiana settler, 97; encouraged emigration of Quakers, 97
Coffin, Levi: 16; aids runaway slaves, 72; and Katie, 73; *Reminiscences*, 75; aids Ede, 77; cousin to Addison Coffin, 97;
Coffin, Vestal, father of Addison Coffin, 97
Colonization, Haiti and Liberia, 34–40
Columbus, Christopher, 10
"Conductors" of above ground railroad, 67
Confederate Congress establishes $500 military exemption fee, 83
Confederate conscription, 82
Confederate prison at Salisbury, NC, 85
Congdon, Ellen L., NY Quaker, helped finance High Point Normal and

Industrial Institute, 101
Contentnea v. Dickenson, case of, 46
Copeland, Henry, of Rich Square Meeting, 79
Cox, Isham, member of Meeting for Sufferings, 79
Craig, Nell, newspaper woman, 108
Creecy, Thomas, rounds up freed slaves, 6
Crenshaw, John B., agent of NC Friends, 83; aids in freeing slaves, 90
Cuba, 11
Curry, Arch, freed slave, dies, papers loaned, 76

D

Davis, James, defends Mary, 51
Declaration of Independence, 4; 30
Dickinson, Contentnea vs, case of, 46
Dickenson will, 46
Dicks, Zachariah: of Cane Creek Meeting, 96; gift of prophecy, 96
Disownment for slaveholding, 53
Doris, brig, takes Quaker Free Negroes to Liberia, 38
Douglass, Frederick, ex–slave, 13
Dunn, Eliza, wife of George C. Mendenhall, 86

E

Eastern Quarterly Meeting, 34
Ede, slave woman, 77
Education of ex–slaves, 99
Edmundson, William, brings Quakerism to North Carolina, 1; 7; disturbed by exploitation of Native Americans and Negroes, 19
Endnotes, 114
Epistle of Advice of 1843, 55; 78
Exemption Act of 1862, 84

F

Fellow, John: accompanies Quaker Free Negroes to Haiti, 34
First Friends Monthly Meeting, 111
Folger, Asa, conducts Quaker Free Negroes to Indiana, 48; "conductor" of above ground railroad, 69
Forster, Josiah, clerk of London Yearly Meeting, 65
Fox, George: brings Quakerism to North Carolina, 1; 7; founder of Quakerism, 19; accused of stirring up slave revolt in Barbados, 19
Frazier, Robert, Quaker and chairman of the board of NCA&T, 107
Freed slaves: put up for sale, 5; convention of, 65; oppose banishment from

America, 65
Freeman, Newlin vs, case of, 50
Freedmen's Bureau:: co-sponsors Quaker school, 99; 107
Freeman (Friedman), Sarah: wills slaves to J. Newlin, 50
Friends free slaves, 3
Friends Freedmen's Association, 108
Friends meetings welcome African-Americans, 112
Friends schools sponsored by New York Yearly Meeting, 99
"Friends Society" credited with aiding integration, 111
Fugitive Slave Act, 76
Fundamental Constitutions of Carolina, 1669, 7

G

Gardner, Delphina: second wife of G. C. Mendenhall, 53; daughter of Barzilla Gardner, an antislavery activist, 86
Garrison, William Lloyd, publisher of *Liberator,* 74
Gaston, Judge William: lawyer for yearly meeting, 31; portrait, 32; 44; 46; *Genius of Universal Emancipation,* 43
Goldsboro, NC, 98
Granville, Lord, 4
Greensboro Daily News, 111
Greensboro, NC, 97; 109
Greensboro Patriot, 42
Guilford College, formerly New Garden Boarding School, 106; 107; 112

H

Haiti, Republic of: 34; Quaker Free Negroes sent to, 34; emigration to, 35; loses appeal, 35
Haley, Alex 11
Hall, Associate Judge John, 48
Hampton, first black member of Greensboro City Council, 107
Hampton Homes, 1965 urban renewal project, 107
Hannah, threatened with slavery, 51
Harris, Obadiah, membership at New Garden delayed, 23
Helper, Hinton Rowan, author of *Impending Crisis,* 73
Henley, Joseph: frees slaves, 3
Henley, Jesse: membership delayed at New Garden Meeting, 24; condemns his own conduct, 24
Henry, Prince, the Navigator, 9
Hertford, NC, site of first Quaker services, 19
Hiatt, John, visits Obadiah Harris, 23

High Point, City of: site of Solomon Blair school 99; 100; buys High Point Normal and Industrial Institute, 101; American Friends Service Committee office, 109
High Point Normal and Industrial Institute: formerly Solomon Blair school, 100; unconsciously segregated, 106
Hill, Roger, 20
Hinson, Josiah, on plantation life, 13
Hobbs, Mary Mendenhall, granddaughter of Richard Mendenhall, 105
Hobbs, President Grimsley, Guilford College, 112
Holden, William, first Lt. Gov. of North Carolina, 16
Hopewell Friends Meeting, Winchester, VA 105
Hubbard, Jeremiah, of North Carolina Meeting for Sufferings, 65
Hunt, Governor Jim, 110
Hunt, Joseph, "conductor" of above ground railroad, 69

I

Illinois, destination for ex–slave refugees, 67
The Impending Crisis, exposé of slavery, 74
Indiana, destination for ex–slave refugees, 67
Indiana Yearly Meeting, Committee on African Concerns, 69
Integration of the schools, 110
Isabella, Queen of Spain, 10

J

Jay, Allen, 105
Jefferson, Thomas, sees contradiction between slavery and Constitution, 4
Jewish community credited with aiding integration, 111
Joe (Jo): kidnapped, 48
Johns, James, admonished by Story over welfare of Indian servants, 20
Johnson, Colonel Richard: intervenes for Joe, 48
Jordan, Joseph, prepares manumission papers, 27
Julius Pringle, schooner: bound for Haiti, arrives arrives in Philadelphia, 59

K

Kennedy, John, American Colonization Society representative, 39
Kennedy, Thomas: visits Haiti, 35; 69; convicted of treason, 85
King, Francis T.: formed Baltimore Association to aid NC Quakers, 98; traveled under pass signed by Lincoln, 98; 106

L

Lane, Harriet, slave, travels under flag of truce, 90
Lane, Lunsford, reports on childhood as slave, 15
Las Casas, Bartolome de, Catholic priest, 10–11
Laughlin, Seth, War Quaker, dies in Confederate prison, 84
Liberator, abolitionist paper, 74
Liberia: "land of liberty," 36; colony for Quaker Free Negroes, 36; waning interest in, 40; Quaker–held Negroes refuse to go (1832), 65
Lincoln, Abraham: considers returning African–Americans to Africa, 36; 81; pass signed by, 98
London Yearly Meeting: admonishes North Carolina Friends to free slaves, 6; favors abolition, 65
Lundy, Benjamin, abolitionist, 43

M

Mace, Benjamin, 58; weary conductor of Quaker Free Negroes, 64
Mace, Jonas: in charge of Quaker Free Negroes, 58; sees refugees off, 62
Manumission papers issued by Joseph Jordan, 27
Manumission Society: organized as bridge between Quakers and other antislavery forces, 41; petitions North Carolina legislature, 42; last meeting held at Marlborough Friends Meeting, 43; 45; 69; 78
Manumissions granted annually, 52
Marlborough Friends Meeting, site of last meeting of Manumission Society, 43
Maroon community of runaway slaves, 16
Massey, Levi Hollowell, sufferings of, 85
McPhail, John, of American Colonization Society, 40
Meeting for Sufferings: defined, 33; 34; 40; 45; 48; 50; declares mission accomplished, 54; 59; 64; 65; 66; 67; 69; 78
Mendenhall, Delphina, poetry of, 88; 92
Mendenhall, George C.: "accidental" slaveholder, 45; helps Joe, 48; disowned for marrying out of meeting, 53; frees slaves in will, 53; 67; special policy toward slaves, 86; emancipates slaves in will, 87; will validated, 90
Mendenhall Inn: possible station on Underground Railroad, 78
Mendenhall, James Ruffin: son of Eliza and George, 86; interferes with freeing of father's slaves, 90
Mendenhall, Nathan: member of Meeting for Sufferings, 40; 64; 69
Mendenhall, Nereus: principal of New Garden Boarding School, 74; pleads for military exemption, 83

INDEX

Mendenhall, Richard: abolitionist and legislator, 45; proprietor of Mendenhall Inn, 78
Mendenhall, William, owns copy of *The Impending Crisis,* 74
Minute of Advice of 1861, 82
Meritorious service required for manumission, 5
Methodist–Episcopal Church South disavows interference with slavery, 56
Moore, Charles, Sheriff of Perquimans County, 5
Moore, Hugh, anecdote about Haiti, 35
Moore, Joshua, manumitted slaves, 5
Moravians fear slave rebellion, 4

N

A Narrative of Some of the Proceedings of North Carolina Meeting on the Subject of Slavery Within its Limits, 54;
Native Americans: welcome runaway slaves, 18; 19; Governor Archdale friendly to, 21
Nautilus, ship, takes Quaker Free Negroes to Liberia, 38; 40
New England Yearly Meeting declares that Quakers will be disowned for slaveholding, 6
New Garden Boarding School: aided by Baltimore Association, 98; transformed into Guilford College, 106
New Garden Friends School, 112
New Garden Monthly Meeting: 4; 14; 22; moves against slavery, 24; encouraged integration of Guilford schools, 110; segregated 111; 112
New Garden, NC, southern terminus of Underground Railroad, 76
New Garden Quaker community, 22
New York Friends welcome Quaker Free Negroes, 71
New York Yearly Meeting of Friends: co–sponsors Quaker school, 99; 100; sells High Point Normal and Industrial Institute, 101; 102;
Newby, Thomas, manumissionist: frees slaves, 3; frees Nacy, 26;
Newlin, John: receives slaves from Sarah Freeman, 50
Newlin v. Freeman, case of, 50
Nicholite religious community, 14
Nicholson, Thomas, writer of abolitionist tracts, 4
Nixon, Phineas: accompanies Quaker Free Negroes to Haiti, 34
Nixon, Sach., frees slaves, 3
Non–Quakers assign slaves to North Carolina Yearly Meeting, 32–33
Norfolk, VA: point of departure for Liberia, 37–40
North Carolina Legislature: petitioned to free slaves, 30; 45
North Carolina public schools, integration of, 111

North Carolina School Boards Association, 110
North Carolina State Archives, 5
North Carolina Supreme Court: Quakers appeal to, 47
North Carolina Yearly Meeting of Friends: 3; admonishes Friends to free slaves, 3; hires lawyers to defend freedmen 5; issues order against buying and selling of slaves by Quakers, 24; adopts weak statement condemning importation of slaves, 24; condemns slavery, 26; offers to send freed slaves to Haiti, 34; *A Narrative of Some of the Proceedings of North Carolina Meeting on the Subject of Slavery Within its Limits,* 54; Epistle of Advice, 55; 1844 letter to monthly meetings, 56; petitions legislature for "extermination of slavery," 66; 78; Minute of Advice, 82; issues certificate of removal, 96;
Northwest Territory: attracts Quakers, 95; map, 95

O

Oberlin College in Ohio, 106
Ohio, destination for ex–slave refugees, 67
Olmsted, Frederick L., on plantation life, 12
Osborne, Charles, organizes NC Manumission Society, 41
Othello, Shakespeare's, 8
Outland, Thomas, "conductor" of above ground railroad, 71

P

Parker, Josiah, assists Quaker Free Negroes in getting to Liberia, 38
Pasquotank County, 6; 96
"Passports" for freed slaves, 92
Payson, Mrs., teacher at Slater Academy, 103
Peale, James, delivers Quaker Free Negroes to Philadelphia, 59
Peck, Harriet, teacher and abolitionist, 53
Peele, Robert, "conductor" of above ground railroad, 71
Penny, defended by Quakers, 51
Perkins, Needham, aids runaway slaves, 77
Perquimans County, 4; 5; 6
Perquimans Monthly Meeting, 1
Philadelphia Friends: aid in Liberian resettlement, 37; discourage immigration of ex–slaves, 59; assist refugees, 60–62
Philadelphia receives freed slaves, 59
Philadelphia Yearly Meeting of Friends: receives protest against slavery, 6; testifies against slavery, 6
Phillips, Henry, 19

INDEX

Plantation life, 12
Portugal and slave trade, 9
Proctor, Billy, fears resale, 73
"Protector of the Indians," 10–11

Q

Quaker Free Negroes: 31; 33; 37; 46; 50
Quaker manumissions declared illegal, 5
Quaker school sponsored by New York Yearly Meeting, 99
Quakers: free slaves, 3; protest slavery to Philadelphia Monthly Meeting, 6; excused from taking oaths and from military service by Governor Archdale, 21; migrate to NC from VA, PA and Nantucket, 21–22; in Philadelphia aid Liberian resettlement, 37; in court, 44; sued for the freedom of two black children, 51; militant antislavery wing, 75; draft-age, hide and flee South, 82; emigrate to West because of slavery, 80, 82; seek Civil War military exemption, 82

R

Racial justice encouraged by Quakers, 107
Radcliff, Samuel, plans to take his family to Haiti, 35
Resettlement in other states, 67
Richmond, IN, 97
Robertson, Joseph, escorts ex-slaves to Liberia, 62
Ruffin, Judge J. 44; in Wayne County Superior Court, 46
Runaway slaves, 72

S

Sally Ann, ship, takes Quaker Free Negroes to Haiti, 34; 35
Saunders, Congressman Romulous: helps free Joe, 48
Schools established by Baltimore Association, 98
Secession, 81
Seminoles, 18
"Separate but equal" in education, 106
Shakespeare's *Othello,* 8
Sherbro Island, off west coast of Africa, freed slaves emigrate to, 38
Shope, Nathaniel, superintendent of Wayne County public schools, 110
Shore, Shelby, member, Yadkin County pubic schools board of directors and member of NC School Boards Association, 110
Slater Industrial Academy for Negroes, Winston–Salem, 103
Slave rebellion feared, 4

Slavery, African, introduced to America, 11
Slaves: African, war prisoners, 11; treatment of, 12–18; ruled to be "property," 31; Quaker–held, hired out, 45;
Smith, Ben L., superintendent of Greensboro public schools, 111
South Africa and apartheid 112
Southern Heroes, 77; 83; 85; 105
Sowle, Patrick, article on Quaker conscripts in Civil War, 84
Spring Monthly Meeting, 50
Springfield, 108
Springfield Monthly Meeting of Friends, 109
"Stations" of Underground Railroad, 75
Stockard, Sally, historian, 86
Story, Thomas, visits Indians, 20
Stowe, Harriet Beecher, author of *Uncle Tom's Cabin*, 12
Supreme Court, decision of 1954, 110
Sutherland, David, citizens petition freedom of, 52
Swaim, George: meets the *Julius Pringle* 59; 64
Swaim, William: editor of *Greensboro Patriot*, 42; ex–Quaker whose actions were influenced by Friends testimonies, 53
Symons Creek Monthly Meeting, 96

T

T. Wingate Andrews High School, merged with William Penn High School, 102
Tappan brothers, oppose colonization, favor abolition, 65
Taylor, John L., Chief Justice of NC Supreme Court, 47
Thornwell, Rev. J. H., preaches on humanity of slaves, 14;
Tomlinson, Allen U., pleads cause of NC Quakers in Richmond, VA, 83
Trent River Monthly Meeting, 96
Tubman, Harriet, on plantation life, 13
Turner, Nat, revolt, 57

U

Underground Railroad, 72–80; 108

V

Vina, New Garden washerwoman aids Underground Railroad, 76

W

Wages paid to freed slaves, 32

Walton, George, frees slaves, 3
War Quakers, 84
Warner, Yardley, Philadelphia Quaker: builder of model village for former slaves, 107; established 30 schools 107; 108
Warnersville, Greensboro, NC, model village for former slaves, 107; 108
Weeks, Stephen B., historian, 96
Western Quarterly Meeting, 24
White, Aaron, rescues emigrants from canal, 39
White, Caleb: frees slaves, 3; requested that Meeting for Sufferings not send recruiters to Eastern Quarter, 40
White, David: agent for Meeting for Sufferings, 59; 65; 69
White, George F., opposes abolitionists, 56
White, Miles: "conductor" of above ground railroad, 71; 91
White, Thomas, frees slaves, 3
Whittier, John Greenleaf: abolitionist, 75; 88
William Penn Foundation, Inc., 102
William Penn High School: 102; on National Register of Historic Places, 102;
Williams, Richard, visits Obadiah Harris, 23
Winslow, Caleb, petition for slave's freedom rejected, 52
Winslow, Clifford, chair of the Perquimans County board of education, 110
Winston–Salem Teachers College, formerly Slater Academy, 104
Winston-Salem State University, formerly Winston–Salem Teachers College, 104
Woody, John W., "white president" of Slater Academy, 104
Woody, Mary Chawner, Slater Academy promoter, 104
Woolman, John: opposes slavery, 3; 7; 8; 14; anti–slavery activist, 22; 75; 108
Woolson, Mrs., teacher at Slater Academy, 103
World Gathering of Friends, 1967, 112
Worth, Daniel: ex–Quaker become Wesleyan Methodist, 55; 74; 79
Worth, Jonathan, governor of NC and ex–Quaker whose actions were influenced by Friends testimonies, 53
Wright, Thomas, assigns slaves to New Garden Monthly Meeting, 51

Y

Young Friends: caravan conducts slaves to freedom in IN, 71

About the Author

Hiram H. Hilty has been in Quaker service in New York, Cuba, Mexico and North Carolina, and is now retired from the faculty of Guilford College. A native of Iowa, he attended the public schools of Missouri. He graduated from Bluffton College and Hartford Theological Seminary and holds the Ph.D. degree in history from Duke University. With his wife, the former Janet Brown, he lives in Greensboro, North Carolina.